GREAT MOMENTS

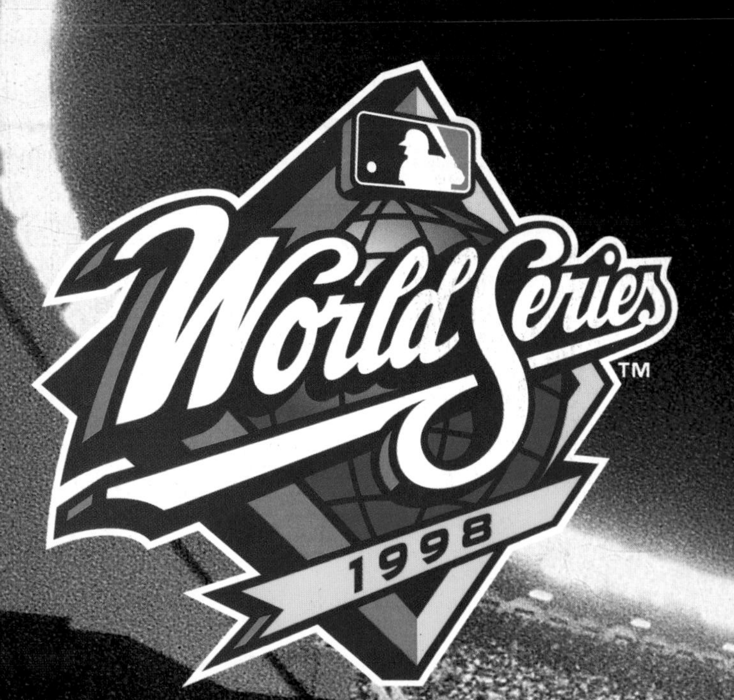
World Series
1998

GREAT MOMENTS

CONTENTS

Woodford Press
660 Market Street, San Francisco, CA 94104
Visit our website at www.woodfordpub.com

David Burgin, Editor
Book design by Jim Santore

Produced in partnership with and licensed by
Major League Baseball Properties, Inc.

Great Moments is an official publication of Major League Baseball

To order additional copies of this, or any other Official Book of the World Series, or for a Woodford Press catalog, please call toll-free, 1-888-USA-BOOK, or 415-397-1853

ISBN: 0-942627-34-2 paper
0-942627-42-3 cloth
First Printing: November 1998
Printed and bound in the United States of America
Distributed to the trade by Andrews McMeel Universal, Kansas City, MO

The 1998 World Series

American League Champion
New York Yankees
vs.
National League Champion
San Diego Padres

RESULTS

Game One, Saturday, Oct. 17, at New York: Yankees 9, Padres 6

Game Two, Sunday, Oct. 18, at New York: Yankees 9, Padres 3

Game Three, Tuesday, Oct. 20, at San Diego: Yankees 5, Padres 4

Game Four, Wednesday, Oct. 21, at San Diego: Yankees 3, Padres 0

Sammy Sosa threw out first ball in Game One.

THE YEAR

Martin F. Nolan

In August, before a game in which the Giants were trying to out-hustle the Cubs to get in the playoffs, San Francisco manager Dusty Baker asked the Chicago outfielder and sudden slugger how he was doing. The reply explained why Baker and everyone else loves Sammy Sosa: "Just tryin' to make the team, Skip, just tryin' to make the team."

Sammy made the team, as did Mark, Cal, Roger, David, Kerry, Ken, Barry, Juan and all the others who made the 1998 season The Year That Was.

Baseball has been subjected to its share of life's stresses over the years. But, as Ted Williams has said, no matter how many tinkerers would presume to mess wtih the game, they can't destroy what happens between the lines. The game outruns any pursuers, a happy Roadrunner outsmarting the avaricious schemes of Wile E. Coyote.

In 1998, any distress was replaced by the fresh breeze of history that cheerfully assaulted records few thought would be broken. Mark McGwire and Sosa disproved the notion home run hitters often wilt in August and September while pitchers still get their rest. Many doubts disappeared in the nanosecond it took Mark McGwire's 62nd home run to travel 341 feet over the left field fence at Busch Stadium in St. Louis.

McGwire's 62nd, shattering the record set by Roger Marris in 1961, provided a shared-by-millions moment in the tribal memory. Many will remember exactly where they were when Steve Trachsel's pitch began its journey. I was in a bar on a Nantucket wharf, where two TV sets flickered, one showing the Yankees-Red Sox game, the other the Cubs against the Cardinals. The bar crowd was quiet, then burst into applause when McGwire hit it out.

McGwire went on to hit 70 homers. Seventy!

A quieter moment occurred at Camden Yards in Baltimore, when Cal Ripken Jr. decided to stop breaking records by taking himself out of the lineup, just another historic moment in a season of historic moments.

If not a perfect season, it had a perfect game pitched by someone with an imperfect body, David Wells, resembling a weekend Saloon League hurler. The Yankees pitcher, who identifies with a portly portsider named George Herman Ruth, blew 'em away in May.

Kerry Wood of the Cubs tied the strikeout record of Roger Clemens with 20, inspiring

T H A T W A S

Mark McGwire's turn in Game Four.

Clemens to pitch as if he wanted another Cy Young Award. In any other season, fans would be focusing on the accomplishments of Ken Griffey Jr., Barry Bonds and Juan Gonzalez.

But baseball is a team sport and, as the World Series proved, what a team! The San Diego Padres, that is. As champagne fizz sprayed the visiting team clubhouse, the air over Mission Way was also intoxicating, as Padres fans saluted their gallant warriors.

The walking wounded were Tony Gwynn, Ken Caminiti and Greg Vaughn. All had lifted the Padres in the regular season over the Giants, Dodgers and Rockies. In the post-season, Kevin Brown, Sterling Hitchcock and Andy Ashby pitched their way through the Astros and the Braves.

The Padres were then swept by a Yankees team still piling up superlatives in the declarative and subjunctive moods. Their record of 114 regular-season victories spoke for itself. Add to that their 11 wins in the playoffs and World Series. And in the "best-ever" debate, the lads in the pinstripes were bystanders. This was a Yankees team without Mr. Braggadocio in the lineup.

They were too good to brag, too efficient, too confident. The bard to sing their praises need not be Red Smith or Grantland Rice, but Peter Drucker or John Kenneth Galbraith, outlining another day at the office. These starless Yankees, with MVPs all over the lineup, played this one for the Henrichs and Woodlings, the Kubeks and Skowrons, not the DiMaggios and Berras, the Ruths and the Gehrigs.

The manager was the star because he set an example. No in-your-face guy, Joe Torre was a quiet analyst. "Even if you're not a baseball fan you know who the Yankees are," he said amid the celebration.

I've spent my life watching pinstripes spin giddily around the bases, but these guys are harder to hate than they are to hit.

In a season of individual achievements, the most towering triumph was a team victory. The Padres and Yankees proved again that baseball is the ultimate team sport, where quiet efficiency trumps trash-talking every day, from April to October, especially in 1998, the season of tribal heirlooms and treasured memories.

Martin F. Nolan is a columnist and political writer for The Boston Globe.

BEST TEAM EVER?

THE RECORD IS CLEAR

Leonard Koppett

The 1998 World Series will be remembered as the one in which the New York Yankees staked their claim as the best team in baseball history.

Their four-game sweep of the San Diego Padres in the Series finally certified what their remarkable regular season had been promisng through six long months. Despite their 114 American League victories, their successful progress through the divisional playoff round and the American League Championship Series, they would not have remained the subject of such all-time comparisons if they had failed to win the World Series itself.

Unfairly and unreasonably, but inescapably, such an ending would have forever diminished their image.

Yet they won the Series, and they won it in four straight. That put the exclamation point on their superiority.

Had they won the Series in six or seven games, their all-time ranking could have been more open to dispute. To be the greatest, they had to win it all, and do it quickly. And you can't win it more decisively than 4-0.

Series sweeps are rare enough — this was the 15th sweep in the 94 World Series played — but putting a Series sweep on top of a .700-plus regular-season winning percentage is rarer still. Only the 1907 Cubs and the Yankees of 1927, l932, 1939 and 1998 did that.

The 1906 Chicago Cubs, who won 116 games and dropped only 36, lost the World Series in six games to their cross-town rivals, the lowly regarded White Sox. The 1954 Cleveland Indians, who set an American League record by winning 111 games (and losing 43), were polished off in four straight by the New York Giants.

The 1927 Yankees, who finished 110-44 for a .714 winning percentage, capped their achievement with a Series sweep over Pittsburgh. That was the year Babe Ruth hit 60 home runs, and the Yankees of 1927 became the team most often cited as the greatest ever.

Among the other usual candidates for a mythical best-ever ranking — the 1902 Pirates (before the modern World Series began), the 1906-1909 Cubs, the 1929-1930 Philadelphia Athletics, the 1936, 1939 and 1961 Yankees, the 1955 Brooklyn Dodgers, the Baltimore Orioles and Oakland A's of the early 1970s, the Cincinnati Reds of 1975

and l976 — only the Yankees of l932, 1939 and 1998 also went on to sweep the World Series.

That's not all. To become world champs, all the teams before 1969 had to lead their leagues and then win only one series against one opponent — in the World Series itself.

The A's, Orioles and Reds of the 1970s had to win a three-of-five League Championship Series to reach the World Series. But the 1998 Yankees had to win a three-of-five (3-0 from Texas) and four-of-seven (4-2 over Cleveland), even after posting their 114-48 record for a .704 winning percentage, which counted for nothing when every post-season series started from 0-0.

Since no other team among these all-time best had to go through such a long and precarious set of extra obstacles to emerge as the ultimate champion, the 1998 Yankees clearly had the best single season ever.

Were the 1998 Yankees also the "best ever" in another sense? If they could play each of these other teams, with all teams in peak form, which team would win? That's a far more speculative question, with no definitive answer possible, of course.

But the mere fact that such arguments can be made establishes the level of greatness of the Yankees of 1998.

Every World Series has its defining historical element. Carlton Fisk's 12th-ining home run identifies 1975. There was Don Larsen's perfect game in 1956, Reggie Jackson's three-homer game in 1977, Bill Mazeroski's final home run in 1960. Willie McCovey's final-out line drive in 1962, the ball bouncing through Billy Buckner's legs in 1986, Babe Ruth's "called" homer in 1932, Kirk Gibson's pinch homer off Dennis Eckersley in 1988, Joe Carter's Series-winning homer for Toronto in 1993, and so forth.

The 1998 World Series did not produce one of those single-moment memories for the ages, but it did provide an even longer-lasting collective
achievement spread over 36 innings — the culmination of a 125-50 season (which is a .714 winning percentage) in this era of extended playoffs.

That achievement, that culmination is a great moment in and of itself, and will never be forgotten.

Leonard Koppett covered baseball for many years for The New York Times. *He is in the writers wing of the Baseball Hall of Fame. His list of books reached 16 with the 1998 publication of* Koppett's Concise History of Baseball.

GREAT MOMENTS

FIELDING

"Catching the ball is a pleasure. Knowing what to do with it is a business."

—Tommy Heinrich

Chris Gomez couldn't field Derek Jeter's leadoff single in the fourth inning of Game Two.

Scott Brosius tries to stretch a single into a double in the fourth inning of Game One.

Rookie Ricky Ledee led off the seventh inning of Game Four with a single. Jim Leyritz tried to pick him off first base.

Joe Girardi looked to pick off a Padres base runner in Game Three.

Quilvio Veras failed to catch Jorge Posada's single to right with one out in the seventh inning of Game One.

Steve Finley fielded Scott Brosius' single in the fourth inning of Game One and threw him out at second.

SAN DIEG

Joyner Drives O'Neill Up the Wall

*A*sk any old baseball man the question and he will give you the answer: "There is always one point in a game when you have a chance to win."

For the Padres in Game Two, the chance came and went in the very first inning when Wally Joyner's apparent two-run double was transformed by Yankees right fielder Paul O'Neill into a really nice-looking third out.

Joyner came to bat with Tony Gwynn at second base and Greg Vaughn at first, and a chance to knock the Cuban expatriate, Orlando "El Duque"Hernandez, off the dais even before he had a chance to clear his throat.

Joyner looked at a ball, then wheeled on a fastball and sent it toward "The Wiz"sign in right field. O'Neill, best known for his strong throwing arm, raced back as if he had rehearsed the play, planted his left foot against the wall, jumped . . . and . . . caught the ball about two feet before it reached the hands of the fans.

Problem averted. Game over, too, although no one knew it at the time.

"That was such a huge play, first baseman Tino Martinez said later in the confident Yankee clubhouse. "One second you're looking at being down 2-0 and the Padres' having all the momentum, and then he just takes it all away."

O'Neill's one lingering memory of this one Series great moment came a few seconds later in the dugout.

"I came off the field, and El Duque came up to me and said something,"O'Neill recalled. "I don't know what it was, but he looked happy."

—-*Ray Ratto*

Game Three got off to a great start for San Diego as Steve Finley made a diving, juggling catch of Chuck Knoblauch's shallow fly to center.

Wally Joyner's textbook slide prevented a double play on Steve Finley's grounder in the second inning of Game Three.

YORK

Derek Jeter advances to second on Mark Langston's wild pitch in the seventh inning of Game One. Jeter eventually scored on Tino Martinez's grand slam homer.

21

NY

PITCHING & THROWING

"Pitching is not a natural act."

—Whitey Ford

David Cone, a 20-game winner in 1998, allowed just two hits and two earned runs in six innings of Game Three.

Chris Gomez starts one of three Padres double plays in Game Two.

David Wells, who grew up in San Diego, pitched just one game—a seven-inning win in Game One.

One of the few highlights of San Diego's 9-3 Game Two loss was three double plays turned by the defense.

Puerto Rico native Ricky Ledee had two of his six World Series hits in Game Four.

A Padres 1998 World Series highlight was Sterling Hitchcock's seven-strikeout, six-inning performance in Game Three.

New York's fortunes in Game Four were helped by two double plays.

Orlando Hernandez, half-brother of 1997 World Series Most Valuable Player Livan Hernandez, gave up just one run and struck out seven in seven innings of Game Two.

Pettitte Keys a Perfect Ending

*F*or the Yankees, this was the last hurdle. For the Yankees, pleasing owner George Steinbrenner meant an all-out try for true and lasting greatness. For the Yankees, there could be no lingering issues when the chase ended. For the Yankees, it meant sweeping the 1998 World Series.

As it was true in two of the previous games, it would not be easy. In Game Four they struggled to parse out Kevin Brown, but in response they had their own pitcher, Andy Pettitte, at his best and most focused. The result, a 3-0 shutout across the jaw of the enemy, was the perfect end to what must be considered a nearly perfect season.

The Yankees had won 125 games when it all ended, losing but 50, for a winning percentage of .714, a number true Yankee fans will never forget. With or without the decimal point.

That Pettitte was the hero in the clinching game was apt, because he was the one Yankee who hadn't been fully engaged by the Series when it began. Indeed, as he readily admitted, his head was not with his body in the two games in New York. His father, Thomas, had undergone double bypass surgery back in Houston six days earlier, helping influence manager Joe Torre's decision to hold out Pettitte until Game Four.

His shining moment, though, came in the second inning, after walking one former Yankee, Jim Leyritz, allowing a single to another, Ruben Rivera, and then walking Chris Gomez with two out. Now he had to get past Kevin Brown. Although a pitcher, Brown was not an automatic out as a hitter, but Pettitte forced him to try to bunt his way on base. Catcher Jorge Posada threw out Brown by a step. It would be San Diego's last chance to put the Yankees on their heels.

—*Ray Ratto*

Andy Ashby won a career-high 17 games in 1998. He started Game Two for the Padres.

Kevin Brown, an 18-game winner during the regular season, was appearing in his second consecutive World Series when he started Game One.

Relief at Last

Appropriately, the last major obstacle to a sweep of the Padres and the championship the Yankees coveted was a figure from their past. With the bases loaded in the eighth inning of Game Four, and San Diego needing three runs to tie, who should step to the plate but Jim Leyritz. The same Jim Leyritz whose dramatic three-run homer in Game Four had reversed the momentum of the 1996 World Series and precipitated New York's comeback.

The Yankees were leading, 3-0, when tiring starter Andy Pettitte walked Quilvio Veras and yielded a single to Tony Gwynn. Righthander Jeff Nelson replaced Pettitte and struck out slugger Greg Vaughn for the second out. But when Nelson fell behind in the count to cleanup hitter Ken Caminiti, manager Joe Torre lifted Nelson in favor of his closer, Mariano Rivera, who was touched for a single on his first pitch.

That left it up to Leyritz, who had enhanced his reputation as a post-season performer with four home runs and nine RBI as the Padres overcame the Astros in the Division Series and the Braves in the National League Championship Series. To date, the highlight of his World Series had been the ovation from the sellout crowd at Yankee Stadium before the first game. He was hitless in his first nine at-bats, with four strikeouts.

But Leyritz had one more chance to right matters for San Diego. He was still miffed from the previous night when manager Bruce Bochy had replaced him behind the plate with a better defender, Carlos Hernandez, denying Leyritz a ninth-inning at-bat against Rivera.

"I wasn't happy coming out," he conceded. "I think, I'm 2-for-2 or 3-for-3 against Rivera when I've faced him. That goes through your mind all the time."

In Game Four Leyritz moved from catcher to first base, an awkward transition that led indirectly to the Yankees' second and third runs. He tried unsuccessfully to beat Paul O'Neill to the bag after fielding a high chop in the eighth inning, prolonging a New York rally. Still, he had the opportunity to eradicate that miscue as well as the Yankee lead.

Rivera had enjoyed an outstanding post-season, holding the opposition without a run in 12 innings spread over nine games. But he had pitched 1 2/3 innings in Game Three when, he admitted later, he didn't have his best stuff. Now the Yankees again needed to squeeze more than an inning from his right arm, and the hard single by Caminiti was an indication he was not in top form.

Still, he challenged Leyritz, who took a fastball on the inside corner for strike two. The batter swung at the next fastball he saw and hit it sharply. But the liner carried all the way to center fielder Bernie Williams, who caught the ball in his tracks for the third out.

The closer made short work of the Padres in the ninth. After yielding a single to his cousin, Ruben Rivera, he induced Hernandez to bounce into a double play and then retired pinch-hitter Mark Sweeney on a grounder to third baseman Scott Brosius for the culmination of an historic season.

The pitcher then dropped to his knees and flung his arms to the sky. It was over.

—*Joe Gergen*

Mariano Rivera saved all three games he pitched in the 1998 World Series.

PADRES

Ailing Ken Caminiti struck out but gave it a valiant effort as he ended San Diego's eighth-inning threat in Game Three.

EMOTION

"You're a pro. Act like one. Do a good job."

— Bobby Thomson, to himself, before hitting a home run off Ralph Branca to give the New York Giants the 1951 National League pennant.

David Wells, who pitched a perfect game earlier in the season, capped off a memorable 1998 by winning Game One.

"El Duque," Orlando Hernandez, struck out seven in seven innings of Game Two.

With men on first and second and one out, Jeff Nelson struck out Jim Leyritz in the eighth inning of Game Two.

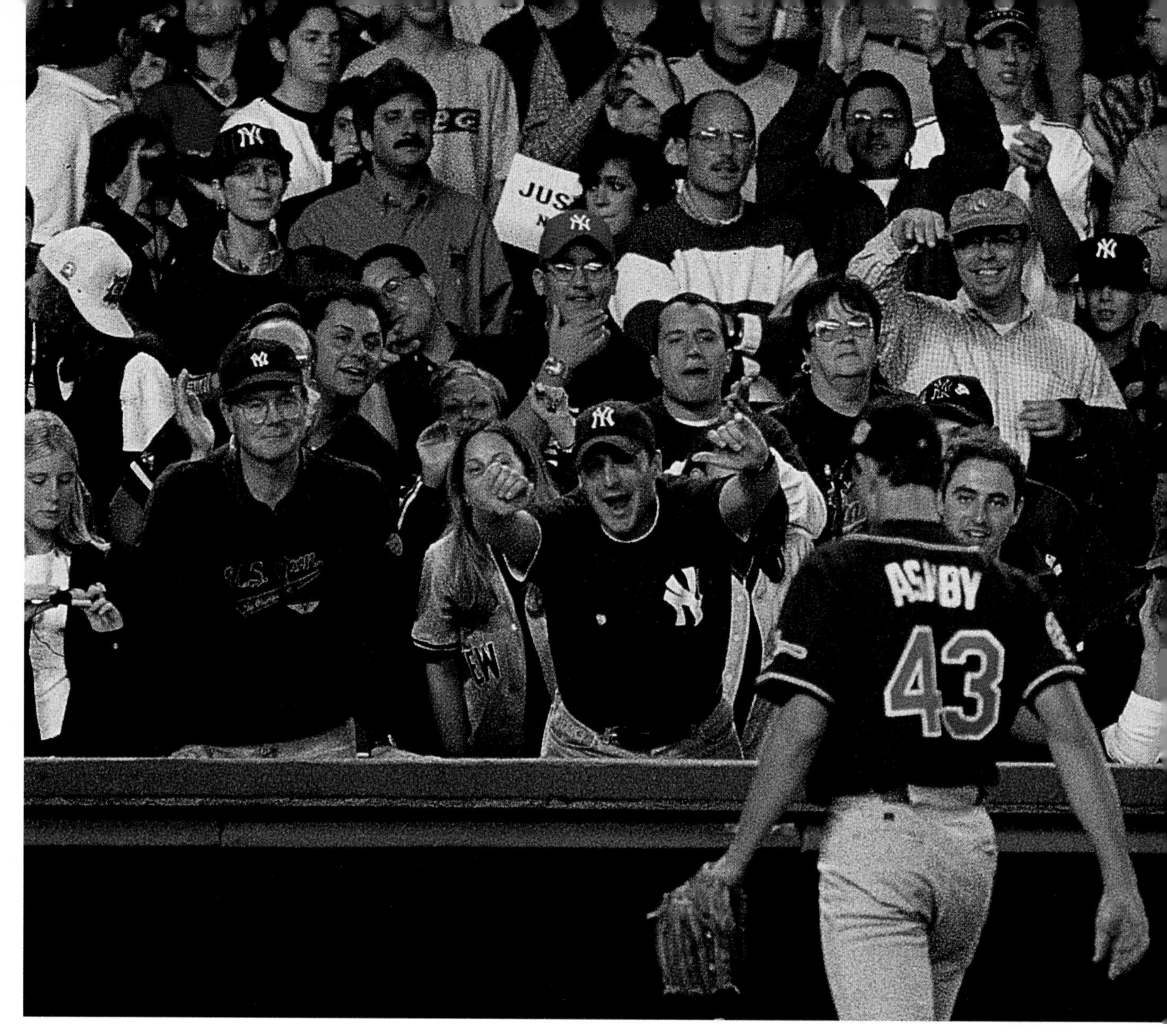

Andy Ashby, like Game One starter Kevin Brown, had the flu when he pitched Game Two.

Greg Vaughn was doubled off second after Ken Caminiti hit into an inning-ending double play in the sixth inning of Game Four.

Joey Hamilton singled to lead off the sixth inning of Game Three. Tony Gwynn's single brought Hamilton home for San Diego's first run.

Yankees Manager Joe Torre discussed a call with home plate umpire Dana DeMuth in Game Four.

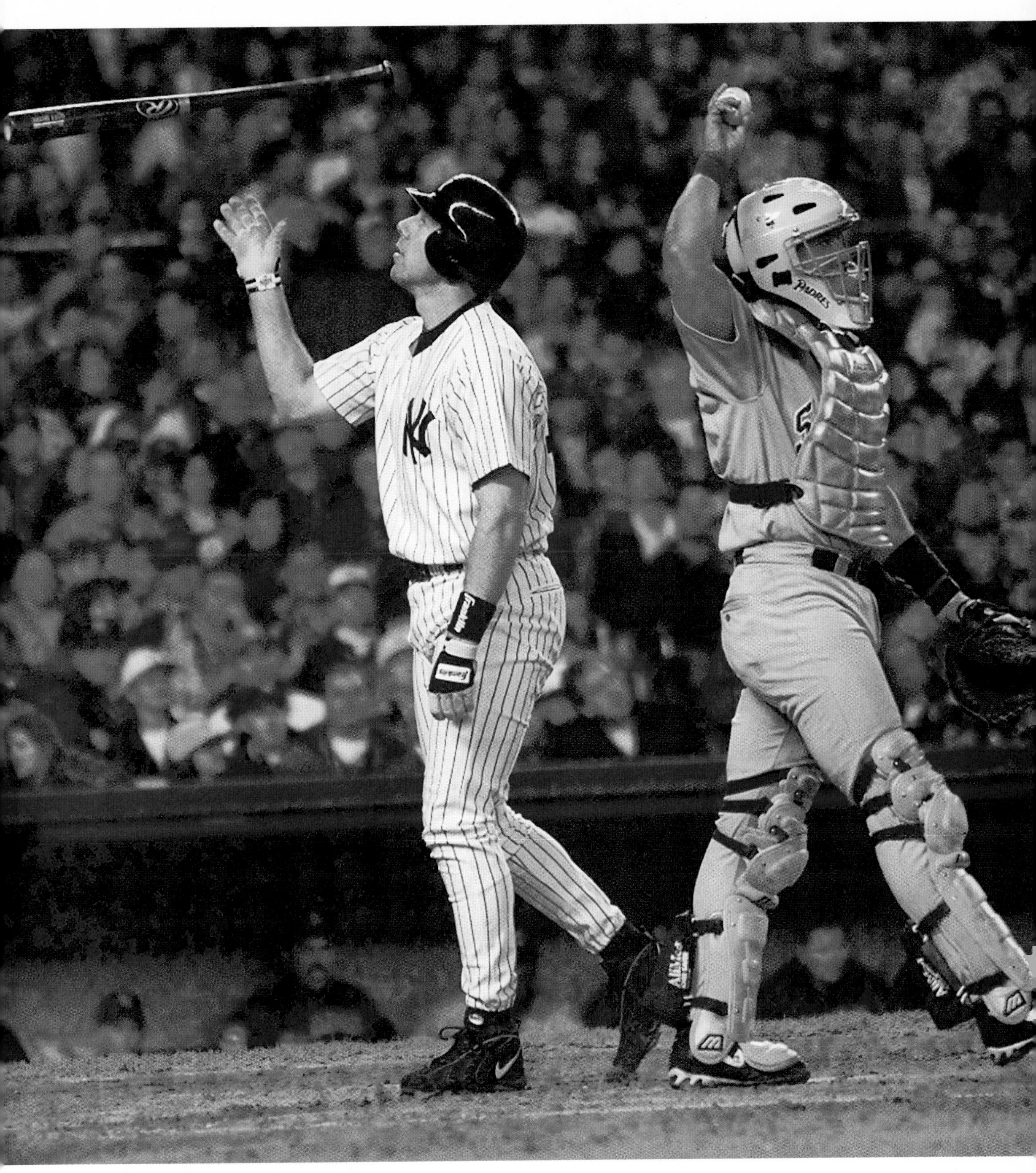

Scott Brosius had one of his few low moments in the World Series when he struck out in the second inning of Game One.

Padres Manager Bruce Bochy (center) and pitcher Kevin Brown did everything they could to win Game Four.

Joey Hamilton's stellar pitching (one run in six innings) wasn't enough for San Diego in Game Three.

A rare sight in 1998: Padres relief ace Trevor Hoffman with a dejected look. This came after he surrendered a three-run homer by Scott Brosius in Game Three.

Randy Myers, a late-season acquisition from Toronto, relieved Dan Miceli in the ninth inning of Game Four.

Joe Torre has won 302 games in his first three seasons with the Yankees. Only Ralph Houk (309 from 1961-1963) has won more than 300 games in his first three years as Yankees manager.

Andy Pettitte, who struggled during the regular season (16-11, 4.24 ERA), shutout the Padres for seven-and-a-third innings in Game Four.

San Diego ace Kevin Brown was pitching on three days' rest in Game Four. He allowed just three runs in eight innings.

Love for the Padres

It didn't take the Padres long to get over their disappointment. They had smashed their heads against the wall. They couldn't break through, and that was all there was to it.

What they did do, though, was stop to smell the roses, to savor the love of their fans even in the face of losing to the New York Yankees' four-game sweep. It started right about the time Trevor Hoffman was walking dejectedly in from the bullpen and noticed the sellout crowd at Qualcomm Stadium, thousands of people on their feet and roaring their thanks.

He tipped his cap slightly and headed into the clubhouse while the Yankees joyously piled atop one another near the mound.

Minutes later, the Padres, hearing the noise, returned to the field to check out the fuss–a long, lingering, thunderous thank-you from a town that had known way too many lean years and now seemed determined to revel in a good one. There was no way to know how many fans were crying, but there were very few dry eyes among the players.

"When I went back out and saw everyone, I almost wanted to apologize," center fielder Steve Finley said through dewy eyes. "The Yankees won the World Series, but only the Padres have this."

Said Mr. Padre, Tony Gwynn, "It's going to be easier this winter even though we lost, because I can't think of anything we could have done differently to change the outcome. To come back out and see how much people appreciated that, well, it was something I won't forget."

Choking back tears, Hoffman was to say later, "This was one of the best moments I've ever had as a player. It's an honor to play before people like this. It makes you proud to be an athlete. These people are for real."

Even the usually flinty-faced Kevin Brown, who pitched admirably in defeat, was more than obligatorily gracious, although he was still having a hard time with a key play in Game Four. The Yankees Paul O'Neill chopped a ball to first baseman Jim Leyritz, who chose to try to make the out himself but got to the bag a nanosecond after O'Neill, at least in the opinions of first base umpire Tim Tschida and the television replays.

Brown leaped in anger and barked at Tschida. Then he got into an argument with second base umpire Jerry Crawford when Crawford tried to calm him down. At the end of the inning, in which New York scored its second and third runs, Brown sarcastically doffed his cap at Tschida.

Afterward, though, Brown had a change of heart, perhaps owing to the goose-bumps cheering from Padres fans.

"I don't apologize for reacting the way I did, because it was just so important," Brown said softly. "But I suppose I should thank (the umpires) for letting me blow off some steam without throwing me out."

In a way, it was the final acknowledgment that the Padres had a special year themselves. The cheering was a great moment that could link San Diego emotionally to its baseball team for years to come.

—*Ray Ratto*

Tino Martinez took a pitch from Kevin Brown in Game Four.

HITTING

"It's very simple . . .Keep your eye on the ball."

— Joe Sewell

Steve Finley's only hit of the World Series came in Game One.

Greg Vaughn's two-run homer in the third inning of Game One tied the game.

Tony Gwynn, playing in his first World Series since 1984, hit a two-out, two-run homer in the fifth inning of Game One to give San Diego a 4-2 lead.

Back to Back

There was a point early in the 1998 World Series when the Padres and Yankees looked like the worthiest of equals. Indeed, it was San Diego's most compelling statement in the entire Series.

That moment came in the fifth inning of Game One, with the score tied, 2-2. Ricky Ledee, the rookie who had taken Darryl Strawberry's place on the Yankee roster after Strawberry was diagnosed with cancer, had doubled home two runs off Kevin Brown in the second inning, but Greg Vaughn had responded with a two-run homer off David Wells in the third, leaving the Yankee Stadium crowd confused by this little plot twist.

They were left even more confused in the fifth, when San Diego made its most forceful statement of the entire Series. Wells had extracted two quick outs from the bottom of the Padres' batting order, but then Quilvio Veras fisted a single into short center, bringing up Tony Gwynn, for years the essence of the Padres franchise.

Wells knew Gwynn's reputation as both a breaking-ball hitter and as a man who worked pitchers deep into pitch counts, so he started him off with a fastball. Gwynn attacked the pitch and drove it off the right field facade, his first post-season home run and San Diego's first lead of the Series.

One pitch later, Wells tried the same thing with Vaughn, who had come within a medical examination of being a Yankee in 1997, and remarkably got the same result as Gwynn, this one a home run to left. In two pitches, the Padres had scored three runs, taken a 5-2 lead and still had their best pitcher in the lineup.

"We were feeling pretty good right then," Gwynn said afterward. "You don't get a lot of chances to get at David Wells, and we had our best guy pitching. We felt pretty pumped right then."

"Doesn't matter," Vaughn said elsewhere in the Padres clubhouse. "We didn't win the game."

—Ray Ratto

Derek Jeter played in his second World Series in three seasons. He hit .353 with six hits in 17 at bats.

Rookie Shane Spencer, whose off-season residence is the San Diego suburb of El Cajon, was playing in his first World Series. Joe Girardi (background) was in his second.

Paul O'Neill's sixth-inning double in Game Four moved Derek Jeter to third base. Jeter scored on Bernie Williams' ground out. Jeter's run was enough for the Yankees to win their 24th World Series.

Tino's Grand Slam

This was developing into another forgettable fall in the career of Constantino Martinez. In the regular season, the first baseman had been everything the Yankees expected after they got him from Seattle in the winter of 1995 to replace popular Don Mattingly.

Yet, as soon as an October came around, and the post-season games began, Tino Martinez withered. The most productive hitter in each of his three seasons in the Bronx, he appeared to shrink in the spotlight with the start of the playoffs. The disappearing act was so pronounced in 1996 that manager Joe Torre benched him in favor of Cecil Fielder during the World Series games in Atlanta, where the Yankees were denied the use of a designated hitter.

Two years later, when Martinez stepped to the plate in the seventh inning of Game One against the Padres, he was the picture of dejection. He had batted an embarrassing .156 for this post-season. And in three years of playoff action for the Yankees, he had managed only one home run and five RBI. Then, with one swing of the bat, in one great moment, it all changed.

Circumstances placed Martinez on center stage. The Yankees had rallied from a 5-2 deficit on Chuck Knoblauch's three-run homer in the seventh inning. With the bases loaded and two out, Martinez faced the third San Diego pitcher of the inning. Lefthander Mark Langston froze the first baseman on a 2-2 fastball in the vicinity of the knees. As a sellout crowd of 56,712 gasped, home plate umpire Rich Garcia made the motion for ball three. The pitch was judged low.

Given a second chance, Martinez drove Langston's next pitch into the third deck in right field. The man's first World Series homer was a big one, the 17th grand slam in Series history. It propelled the Yankees to a 9-6 victory and inspired fans to chant ``Tee-no, Tee-no." All had been forgiven.

``I haven't done much," Martinez conceded after the game, ``but . . . I knew eventually I'd come up in a big situation and get a big hit to help the team. It's a big relief . . ."

Yankees manger Joe Torre would not say he was worried. The Yankees had won the opening game, and Torre looked anew at Tino as found money.

—Joe Gergen

Chili Davis drove in the second run in the seventh inning of Game Three. Ken Caminiti booted Davis' grounder enabling Shane Spencer to score.

The stress of the regular season and National League playoffs caught up with Ken Caminiti during the World Series. Playing in pain, he hit just .143.

Jorge Posada singled in the seventh inning of Game One and scored on Chuck Knoblauch's home run.

Knoblauch's Redemption

It is a tradition of the Series that the first time a manager pokes his head out of the dugout, he is about to make a move that will enrage half the population.

And so it was San Diego manager Bruce Bochy's misfortune, then, that his starting pitcher in Game One hit empty before Yankee manager Joe Torre's starter did. Brown had been flighting both the flu and Yankees hitters' maddening tendency to wait for the right pitch. By the end of the sixth inning, Brown had thrown 100 pitches, the barometer for fatigue in the big leagues. He also had a knot on his left shin from a Chili Davis liner in the second inning.

"Kevin was getting close to the end," Bochy would inform the media mob later. "We decided to let him go out for the seventh, and if he scuffled at all, we'd go get him."

Brown "scuffled." After a routine groundout by Scott Brosius, Brown gave up a sharp single to Jorge Posada and then walked rookie left fielder Ricky Ledee, who was so happy to just to be in the 1998 World Series at all that he thanked manager Torre before the opening game just for putting him into the lineup.

At that point, Bochy made his move. It was too early for reliever supreme Trevor Hoffman, too dicey a jam for starter Joey Hamilton, and a bad spot for lefty Randy Myers, because the man on deck was right-handed hitting Chuck Knoblauch, the very same who had earned the wrath of all New York with an incomprehensible gaffe covering first base in a playoff game. So Bochy stuck out his right arm, and in came Donne Wall.

Wall never had a chance. The pitching gods simply were not with him. He missed badly twice, and his third pitch to Knoblauch should have. Knoblauch hit a high fly ball that hugged the left field line and dropped into the second row of seats, tying the game. With the blow he earned his release from a stretch in New York City's dog pound.

It was so uplifting for Knoblauch, in fact, that he uncharacteristically screamed his joy toward the heavens as he hit home plate. One great moment. And The Gaffe was gone.

—*Ray Ratto*

Paul O'Neill has played in three World Series, two with the Yankees and one with the Cincinnati Reds. He's been on the winning end all three times.

Tony Gwynn had two hits in Game Three. He scored one of the Padres' three runs in the sixth inning.

An MVP Performance

A year earlier he had been the weakest hitter, statistically, on the worst team in the American League. For those who contend that putting on the Yankee pinstripes makes a player better, Scott Brosius evolved into Exhibit A during the course of the 1998 season. His .300 average and 98 RBI batting at the bottom of the batting order led teammate Derek Jeter to suggest Brosius was the club's MVP.

What a turnaround that represented for the third baseman who had struggled to bat .203, with 41 RBI, for the last-place Oakland A's. Not even the Yankees' management believed he was more than a stopgap at a position where incumbents Wade Boggs and Charlie Hayes were let go and prospect Mike Lowell was deemed not ready for the majors. New York traded pitcher Kenny Rogers for Brosius in November of 1997.

Ironically, the Yankees thought they had dealt Rogers to the Padres for Greg Vaughn in mid-summer, but then called off the trade when outfielder Vaughn failed to pass their physical. Vaughn returned to San Diego, where he amassed 50 home runs in 1998 and was a major factor in the team's drive to its first World Series appearance in 14 years. Rogers enjoyed a 16-victory season with the improved A's.

The aborted trade, Padres' general manager Kevin Towers cracked on the eve of the playoffs, "worked out for all three clubs."

It certainly worked out for the Yankees. Within minutes after the Padres took a 3-0 lead over New York in Game Three, Brosius commenced his team's comeback with a solo homer leading off the seventh inning. After yielding one more hit, San Diego starter Sterling Hitchcock was replaced by Joey Hamilton, and the Yankees scored a second run. By the time Brosius came to bat in the eighth, the pitcher was Trevor Hoffman, the most feared closer in the National League, and a man with 53 saves who had blown only one chance for a save all season.

There were two runners on, one out, the count 2-2, when Brosius slammed a 2-2 pitch 424 feet, a home run over the center field fence at Qualcomm Stadium. It was only the second time he had ever batted against Hoffman, the pitcher with the all-world change-up. The previous time was in the All-Star Game and Brosius had struck out. Brosius thus became the 10th Yankees player to account for at least two homers in a World Series game and the first since Reggie Jackson's celebrated trifecta in the 1977 finale.

Brosius was voted the Series MVP.

With his second homer, Brosius pumped his fists in celebration as he rounded first base and acted as if he were a kid rather than a 32-year-old adult.

No wonder. Such World Series heroics are commonplace only in the fantasy games played by youngsters.

"This is something you dream about," Brosius was to say later, still grinning. "I've done this a hundred times in my backyard."

—*Joe Gergen*

RUNNING & SLIDING

"I dress slow. I walk slow. I even sit slow. When I get on the field, I'm fast."

— Hall of Famer Lou Brock

Derek Jeter charged from first to third on a Paul O'Neill double in the sixth inning of Game Four, setting up the first of two Jeter scores.

Padre center fielder Steve Finley found nothing but frustration at the plate during the Series. By the eighth inning of Game Two, he had only one hit.

Derek Jeter scored twice in Game Four, on a sixth-inning grounder by Bernie Williams and on a Scott Brosius single in the eighth.

Left fielder Ricky Ledee, thwarted in his attempt to steal third base in the second inning of Game Two, nontheless wound up with a .600 batting average for the Series.

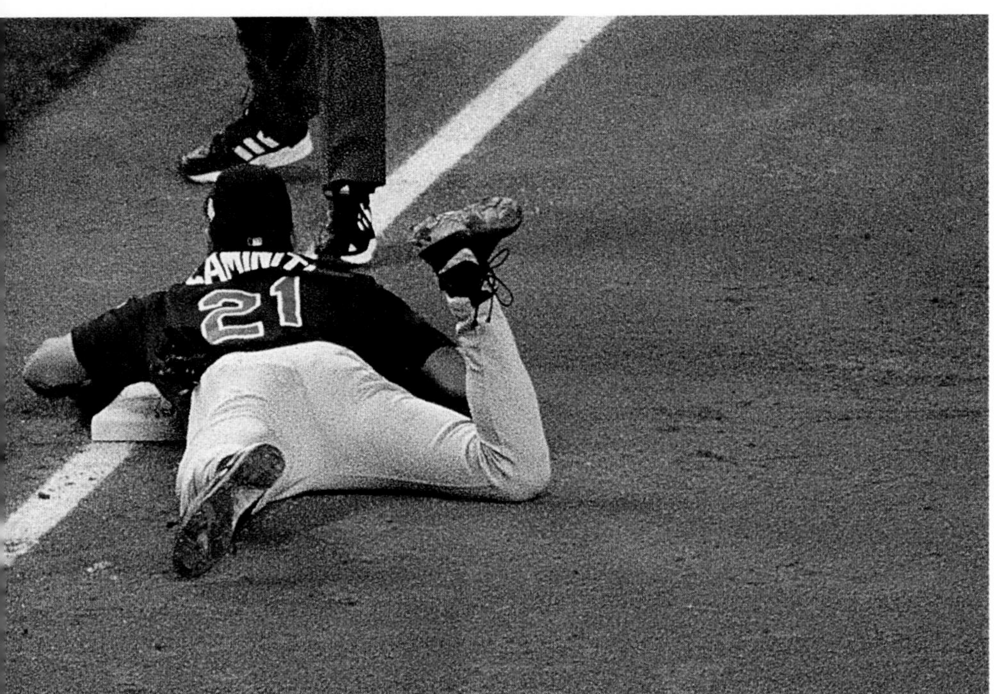

Center fielder Ruben Rivera managed three hits during the Padres' futile attempts to score in Game Four.

18

The Yankees out-hit the Padres only 9-7 in Game Four, but by the seventh inning the Padres were completely run down.

Tony Gwynn tried everything, including hitting .500 for the Series and sliding (safely) into first in the sixth inning of Game Four.

Paul O'Neill, who drew a walk off Randy Myers in the eighth inning of Game Three, continued his tour of the base path when Scott Brosius hit a home run off Padres reliever Trevor Hoffman.

Yankees starter Andy Pettitte kept catcher Joe Girardi alert in the fourth inning of Game Four, but Pettitte still managed to throw seven-and-a-third scoreless innings before relievers took over.

Tino Martinez was intentionally walked in the eighth inning of Game Four to load the bases with one out. He never scored — but two other Yankees did.

Even though first-baseman Jim Leyritz found the bag in time to get Bernie Williams out in the eighth inning of Game Four, the play allowed Paul O'Neill and Derek Jeter to advance to scoring positions.

Derek Jeter was the first of four Yankees to cross home plate after Tino Martinez nailed his seventh-inning grand slam off Padres reliever Mark Langston in Game One.

Leading off the eighth inning of Game One with a single, Tony Gwynn tried to spark a Padres comeback, but Chuck Knoblauch tagged him out after Padre Greg Vaughn hit into a fielder's choice.

CELEBRATION

"I reminded Tug that a lot of photos would be snapped after the last out. We agreed he'd wait until I got there to jump on top of him."

—1980 World Series MVP Mike Schmidt on his plan with Philadelphia Phillies teammate Tug McGraw following the last out of Game Six.

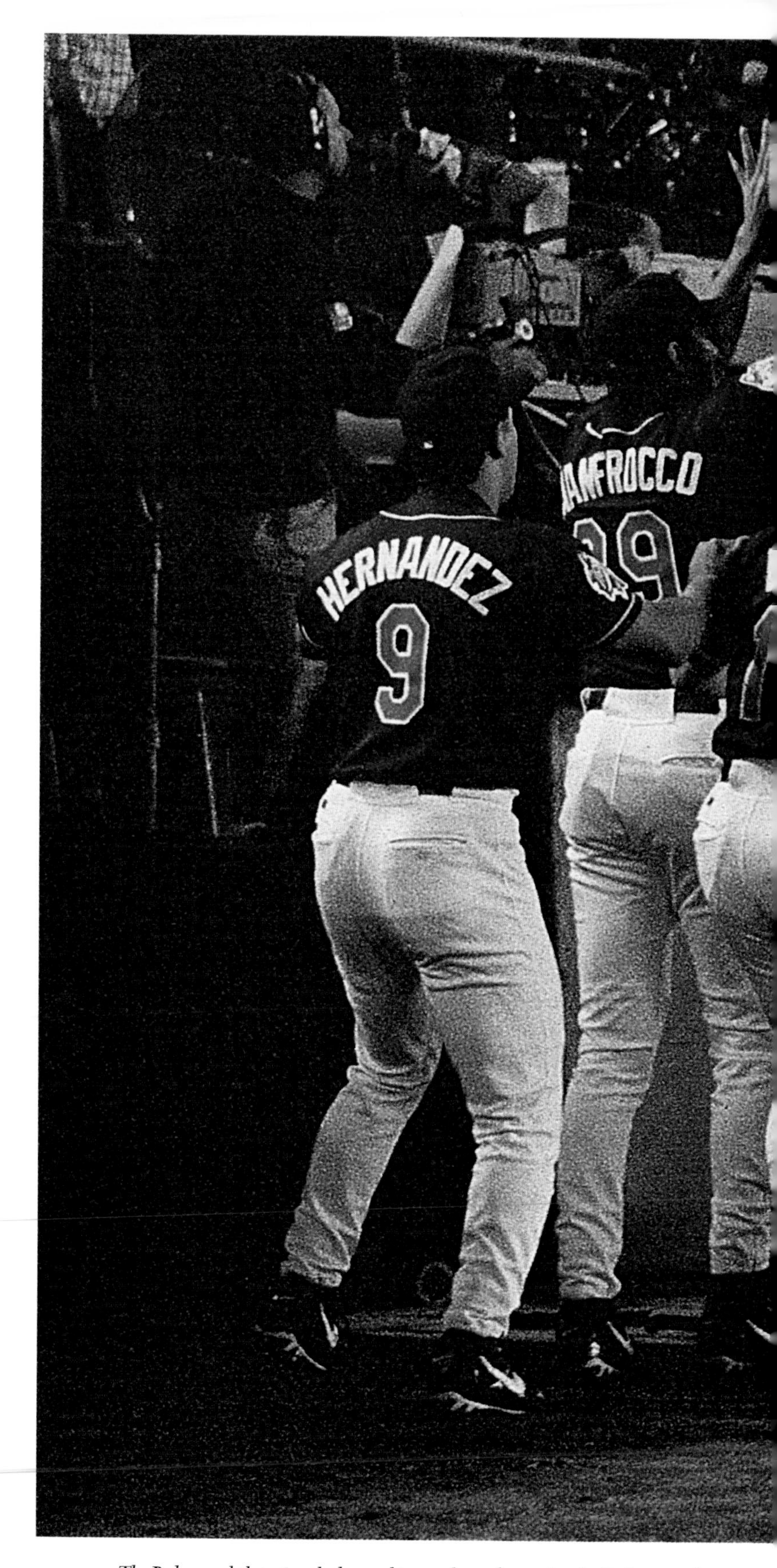

The Padres and their fans had something to shout about after the Padres scored a run in the eighth inning of Game Three to move within a run, 5-4, of the Yankees.

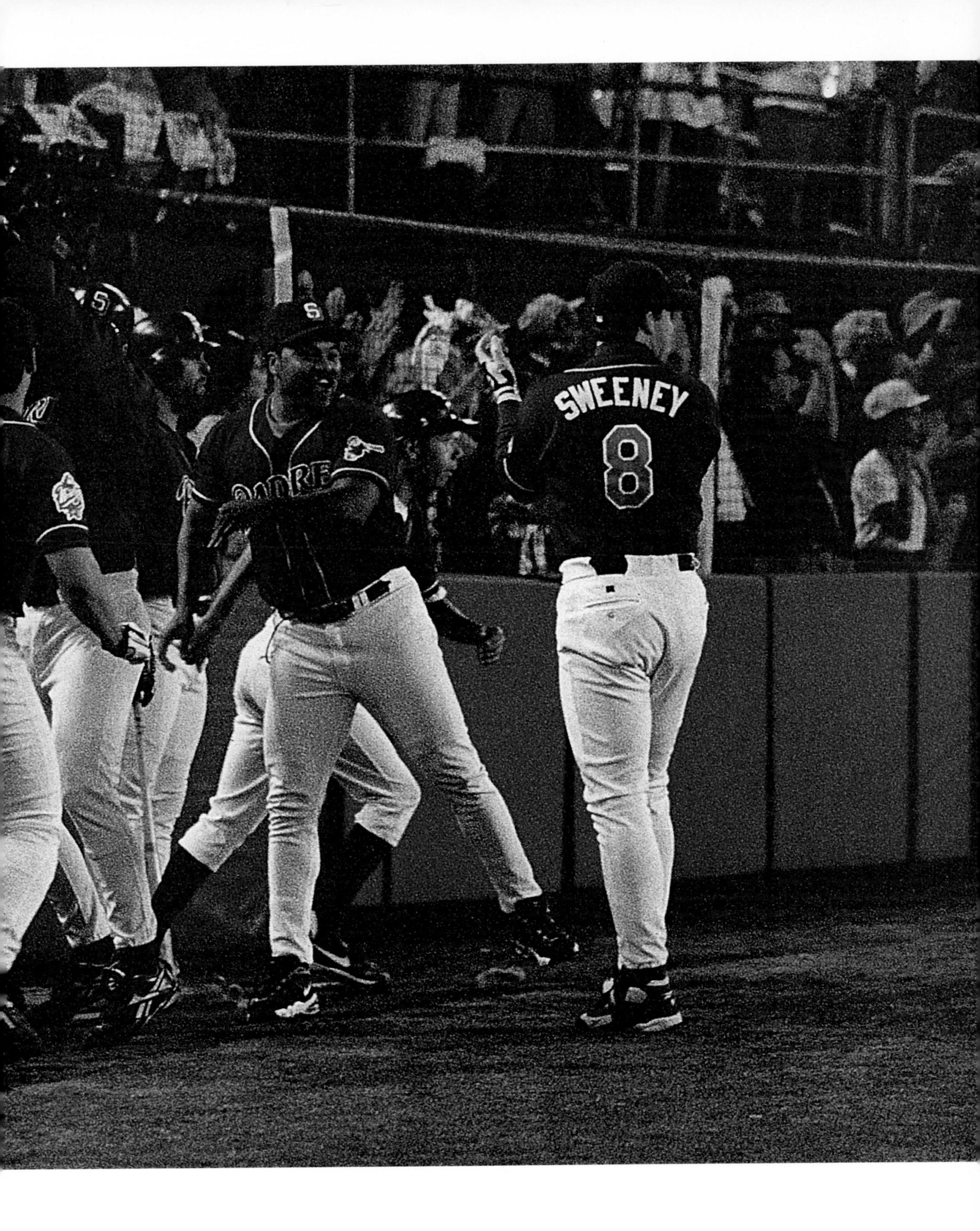
SWEENEY
8

Jeff Nelson, a member of the 1996 World Champion Yankees team, struck out two in preserving New York's Game Two win.

Bernie Williams' two-run homer in Game Two gave the Yankees a 4-0 lead after just two innings.

Derek Jeter (center) and Chili Davis scored ahead of Tino Martinez, whose seventh inning grand slam homer in Game One was the margin of victory.

World Series MVP Scott Brosius homered twice in Game Three, including a three-run game-winner off Trevor Hoffman.

Joe Torre is the first native New Yorker to manage the Yankees. He's also the fourth (joining Yogi Berra, Dallas Green and Casey Stengel) to manage the Yankees and the Mets.

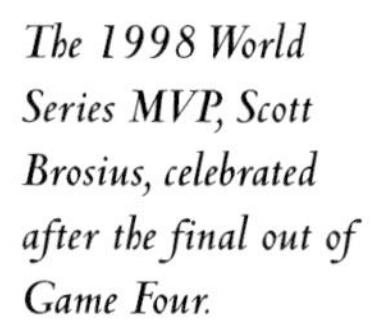

The 1998 World Series MVP, Scott Brosius, celebrated after the final out of Game Four.

NEW YORK
NEW YORK
Franklin

Ex-New York Yankee Jim Leyritz, a key acquisition by San Diego from Boston in mid-season, was one of many Padres who showed their appreciation to the fans after Game Four.

Outfielder Mark Sweeney and his Padres teammates thanked the San Diego fans for their support after Game Four.

Darryl Strawberry, who missed the World Series because he had cancer surgery, received a warm welcome at the parade. Sitting next to Strawberry was his wife, Charisse.

NATIONAL LEAGUE

TONY GWYNN FINDS MONUMENT PARK

Mark Kreidler

On the day before the first game of the 1998 World Series, a man boarded the subway out of Grand Central Station in Manhattan, got off at 161st Street in the Bronx, and walked into Yankee Stadium for the first time in his life. Once inside the gates, he strode out to Monument Park with his 16-year-old son and stood slack-jawed, a genuine fan awed by the sight.

And the thing that made it a great moment was that, in a different circumstance, this particular man might someday have had a plaque in Yankee Stadium to call his own.

Tony Gwynn made it back to the World Series just in time. Now 38 years old, on the far side of a Hall of Fame career that will ultimately include 3,000 hits, at least eight batting titles and 14 All-Star Game appearances, it took Gwynn 14 years to get from his first Series to his second. But make no mistake, it was worth it.

It was worth it to Gwynn, a lifetime .339 hitter who has somehow stitched his remarkable career into the fabric of some forgettable San Diego teams over the years. And it was worth it to the World Series, which received what may have been a final dance across the national stage by one of its classiest hoofers.

"I've never been happier than this year, because we were winning," Gwynn said before the Series began. "It means a lot at this stage of my career to have another opportunity to take that next step."

It was a graceful step, however bittersweet the experience as a whole. While his Padres were busy being cut down by the Yankees, one of the great teams in baseball history, Gwynn did what came naturally, banging out hits and doing it in a San Diego uniform. He finished with a .500 batting average and such respect from those who follow the Yankees that he earned their ultimate compliment: He would have looked good in the pinstripes.

The historical contrast at play here was almost too stark to describe. Suggest the Yankees to any sentient baseball fan, and what comes back is a torrent of names that trigger both memory and emotion: Babe, Lou, Whitey, Mickey, Yogi, Thurman, Goose, Reggie.

The Padres? It's just the one man. Tony Gwynn is the man. He's the franchise. In an era of shifting loyalties and the inevitable effects of free agency, Gwynn at times over his 17-year career seemed to make headlines by not doing anything — by electing to sit still.

It isn't as uncomplicated as it sounds. When the Padres went to the World Series for the first time in their history, in 1984, a wide-eyed Gwynn was in his first full season in the big leagues. He fully believed, as he has admitted, that he'd be back in the Fall Classic soon — perhaps even the next year.

Instead, the Padres plunged into mediocrity, with an occasional glimmer of promise. And Gwynn — at times an anomaly on the team because of his routine excellence — found himself repeatedly urged to jump to a better situation. His father, Charles, begged Gwynn to leave via free agency during a conversation they had in 1993.

Two days after that, Charles Gwynn died unexpectedly. His son ultimately chose to remain in San Diego, where his family, his loyalty and his baseball interest lay. And, late enough in this game within the game, Tony Gwynn reaped a windfall from that decision.

"There isn't a day that goes by that I don't think about how happy (my father) would have been since 1994, when we really started rebuilding the team," Gwynn said.

That building process, under current Padres owner John Moores, paid off in a post-season appearance in 1996 and the National League pennant in 1998, when Gwynn and his teammates defeated a pair of 100-win teams, Houston and Atlanta, in the playoffs.

And Gwynn got his money's worth in the Classic itself, stroking a two-run homer off New York's David Wells in Game One, collecting two hits and driving in a key run in Game Three, and electrifying the home crowd in Game Four with a slide into first base to beat Tino Martinez's diving tag for an infield single.

He smiled, shook hands, accepted appreciative applause almost every time he came to bat, including a gracious ovation from the notoriously tough Yankees fans in Game One. He signed autographs and was the virtual team spokesman through a Series of demoralizing defeats.

"He's everything you've heard about him," said Padres hitting coach Merv Rettenmund, "and then some."

It was classic Gwynn, and it was worth savoring. Gwynn was coming out of a 1998 season in which a variety of ailments, including a painful Achilles injury, limited him to 127 games and a .321 batting average — a career year for some, a disappointment for the man hailed as the best pure hitter in baseball since Ted Williams.

It was worth savoring, because who knew whether the world would see Tony Gwynn on the national stage again? Had he worn Yankees pinstripes for the whole of his career, people might be making the trek to Monument Park in centerfield to study Gwynn's history. Instead, it took the man 17 years just to find Yankee Stadium.

Not a moment too soon.

Sports columnist Mark Kreidler of The Sacramento Bee *covered Gwynn and the Padres for* The San Diego Union-Tribune.

HARRY HAD IT RIGHT

Steve Daley

Television images of the 94th World Series opened in vivid blues and greens as the best baseball season in memory wound up a New York-San Diego affair. On Oct. 17, the inevitable television blimp floated in the night sky above Yankee Stadium, where the game's most storied franchise had engaged in this endeavor 34 times in this century.

In the glare of Fox Television cameras, the old stadium conveyed the weight of its history, with the three tiers of howling New Yorkers looming above a San Diego Padres team that never looked comfortable.

First, your basic TV rituals: Chicago Cubs' outfielder Sammy Sosa wore a blue jacket and a necktie to throw out the first pitch in Game One, and why not?

Fox announcers Tim McCarver and Bob Brenly.

The family of Yankees slugger Roger Maris donned the same shade of blue in the second game, smiling as they wheeled slowly in the long-awaited welter of New York adulation. This year, Maris and his 61 homers made a comeback as surely as the game itself, tugged along by Sosa and his mythic companion, Mark McGwire, who did his first-pitch bit in San Diego before Game Four.

But this was all about the Yankees, one more time. The team that has spent the most time playing October baseball has generated decades of compelling television pictures. For most of us, after all, the bulk of baseball memory plays out in film and video images.

In the black-and-white 1950s there was Yankees pitcher Don Larsen leaping into the arms of Yogi Berra after a perfect game, and Brooklyn's Jackie Robinson sliding past the Yankees catcher, stealing home.

In 1963, a Dodgers rotation of Sandy Koufax, Don Drysdale and Johnny Podres unmasked years of Yankee dominance, dispatching New York hitters back to their dugout in a four-game sweep.

A year later, with the Yankees about to dissolve into a decade of mediocrity, there was still Whitey Ford and Maris and Yogi. And there was Mickey Mantle, chasing a Maris home run in Game Six by rattling a Barney Schultz knuckleball off the right-field facade against the St. Louis Cardinals.

When the Yankees returned to prominence in the 1970s, television gave us Reggie

Jackson launching three preposterous home runs into the Bronx night, breaking down a trio of Los Angeles pitchers on three successive first pitches in Game Six.

In this year's short-lived but compelling affair, Fox broadcasters Joe Buck, Tim McCarver and Bob Brenly provided the script for another Yankees triumph, negotiating around the pictures with plenty of New Age software — "Hit Zones" in blue and red, and "Super Shots" and "Outfield Hits By Direction."

Despite the sweet season, national television ratings for the four-game set were slightly lower than in 1997, although every other viewer barometer—the league playoffs and the local TV markets—showed fans coming back to the game in living rooms and sports bars, as well as through the turnstiles.

The ratings could have been linked to a simple reality: By the time the Series moved to San Diego's Qualcomm Stadium for Games Three and Four, the images were mostly those of Yankees inevitability.

San Diego's hopes evaporated with three-run leads, but television offered an array of great faces: Torre as implacable as a Vatican sovereign; pitcher Orlando Hernandez — "El Duque"— evoking memories of Boston's Luis Tiant, turning his eyes away from the hitters as he rolled into his windup.

On the San Diego side, there stood steely-eyed Kevin Brown staring down an umpire, pitching coach Dave Stewart showing the strain, and formerly invincible relief pitcher Trevor Hoffman nibbling on his glove, wondering why.

In this vintage season, baseball and television lost Chicago Cubs announcer Harry Caray. For more than 40 years Caray brought his broadcast magic to Wrigley Field, to the South Side of Chicago and the White Sox, to Oakland, and to his hometown of St. Louis.

To the dismay of peevish managers and thick-fingered infielders, Caray saw the game the same way the fan does. And, laughing all the way, he raised the same questions a fan would pose.

Harry might have grumbled into the microphone when Padres manager Bruce Bochy decided reliever Donne Wall was better suited to address the New York lineup in the seventh inning of Game One than starter Kevin Brown.

But he would have loved the inspired play of Yankees third baseman Scott Brosius, the grit of Tony Gwynn and the not-dead-yet enthusiasm of the Padres crowd as the sweep marched forward.

Whatever happened to blasé West Coast baseball fans, anyway?

Caray viewed it all with a fan's straightforward perspective. "How," he once asked famously, "can a young fellow from Mexico lose a ball in the sun?"

So, along with the 1998 home-run chase and those 125 Yankees victories, baseball fans will long remember Caray's one-liners, his rumpled, smiling presence and his seventh-inning renditions of "Take Me Out to the Ball Game."

Harry had it right. Even on television, you can't beat fun at the old ballpark.

Uncle Miltie.

Steve Daley is a former columnist for The Chicago Tribune.

BEING NEW YORK IS BASEBALL (OR, BASEBALL IS NEW YORK)

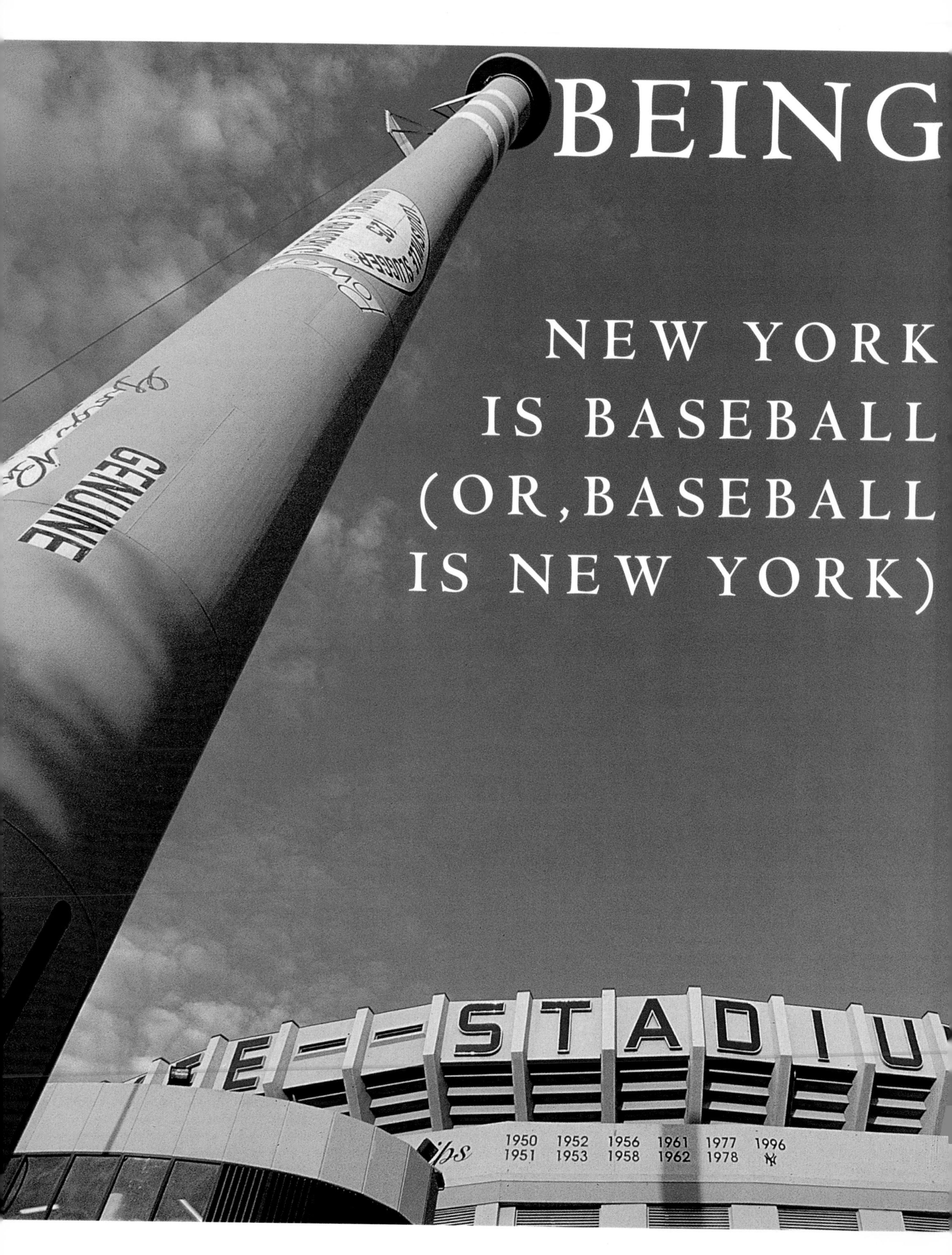

Joe Gergen

Babe, The Iron Horse, Joe D., Willie, Mickey and The Duke
Yogi, The Meal Ticket, Pee Wee
The Scooter, the Barber and Big Newk
Hit Sign Win Suit, Campy, Moose
Poosh 'Em Up, Ol' Reliable, Hug
Coogan's Bluff, Ballantine Blast, Goose
Master Melvin, Tom Terrific, Tug.

Forget Cooperstown for a moment. There is compelling evidence that anyone wanting to understand the history of baseball should start in old New York. Baseball was the very first City Game, created, organized and promoted by a trio of residents whose families had emigrated from England. The game remains rooted in all five boroughs to this day.

Alexander Cartwright, a New York surveyor and draftsman, drew up the rules of modern baseball, set the bases 90 feet apart and divided a game into nine innings. He also formed the Knickerbocker Base Ball Club, the first amateur team which, faced with a growing shortage of open land in Manhattan, traveled by ferry across the Hudson and appropriated a cricket pitch at the Elysian Fields in Hoboken, N.J.

Among the spectators drawn to the Knickerbockers games was Henry Chadwick, a Brooklyn music teacher so smitten by the action he devised the scoring system and the box score, compiled the first printed rule book, wrote a series of instructional books on the sport and covered baseball exclusively for several New York newspapers. His gravestone at Greenwood Cemetery in Brooklyn is topped by a mammoth replica of a baseball, the gift of pioneer pitcher and sporting goods magnate Albert Spalding.

The Knickerbockers also piqued the interest of Harry Wright, a New York jeweler and son of a professional cricket player. In 1858, he joined the team as an outfielder and remained a member until 1865 when he was hired as cricket instructor by a club in Cincinnati. One year later, he founded the Red Stockings. After signing some of the finest players in the East — including his brother George — to the first professional contracts, he led the team on a national tour in 1869. They won 57 games, lost none.

New York's influence has been just as formidable in the 20th century. Of the 94 World Series that have been staged between the champions of the National and American leagues, beginning in 1903, at least one team from the Big Apple has participated in more than half. The 1998 victory by the Yankees was the 24th by that franchise in the Fall

Classic and the 32nd overall by a New York team. The Giants accounted for five, the last in 1954, the Mets two and the Brooklyn Dodgers claimed their only title in 1955. Of all the cities where baseball has taken hold, St. Louis is a distant second with nine championships.

Numbers alone don't tell the full story of New York's immersion into the sport. Major league ballparks have been erected in Manhattan, Brooklyn, the Bronx and, most recently, Queens. The only borough slighted is Staten Island, which produced the player who hit the most celebrated homer in baseball history. Bobby Thomson, the Staten Island Scot, beat the Dodgers with his ninth-inning blast on behalf of the Giants in the third and final National League playoff game. The date was Oct. 3, 1951.

Almost 50 years later, earwitnesses can remember the circumstances of that hit off Ralph Branca and recall the broadcast of Russ Hodges: "The Giants win the pennant, the Giants win the pennant . . . ". It continues to be a point of reference for generations of novelists — a landmark moment in sports and America's consciousness." The Shot Heard Round the World" resonates today.

To older New Yorkers, that era remains the golden age of baseball, a time when three metropolitan teams vied for the attention and loyalty of area residents, sometimes dividing families in the process. In her best-selling memoir of growing up on post-World War II Long Island, Doris Kearns Goodwin ties her youth to the fate of the Dodgers and uses a term familiar to their fans as her title: *Wait Til Next Year*. You could walk past a row of houses on a New York street and not miss a pitch on the radio.

The Giants and Dodgers fled to the West Coast in 1957, darkening the New York City summer. Recognizing the political fallout of the defections, Mayor Robert Wagner assigned Bill Shea to find a replacement, and shortly thereafter the Mets were born as a National League expansion team. All New York, and much of the country, celebrated when the bumbling toddler grew up all at once and concluded its first winning season with a division title, a pennant and a World Series championship. These were the "Miracle Mets" of 1969.

Although John Lindsay wasn't much of a baseball fan, strategists credit his re-election as mayor in part to the champagne-dousing he received from the Mets in their Shea Stadium clubhouse after Cleon Jones recorded the final out. Another mayor, Rudolph Giuliani, seemed to hitch his political wagon to the Yankees as a symbol of the city's renaissance. He also was one of the lobbyists for a new stadium to house the Yankees on the West Side of Manhattan.

Ebbets Field and the Polo Grounds are fond memories. Shea Stadium still seems new compared to Yankee Stadium, which survived into the 1998 season, and with it the tradition to which baseball-crazed New Yorkers cling. Whatever happens, the idea of Yankee Stadium is as comforting as the sight of Joseph Paul DiMaggio, still introduced as the "Great Living Ballplayer" nearly half a century after his last game.

Yankee Stadium is where a Brooklyn youngster and Giants fan named Joe Torre sat in the upper deck and watched Don Larsen pitch a perfect game against the Dodgers. That was in 1956 in the last "Subway Series." And it is where Torre sat in the home-team dugout — 42 years later — and saw David Wells pitch a perfect game for his Yankees.

As so many all around the town are fond of saying, "Only in New York."

Casey, Whitey, Dusty
Oisk, Doc, John McGraw
Skoonj, Mandrake, Rusty
King Kong, Catfish, Straw.

Joe Gergen is a sports writer for Newsday.

The real Joe DiMaggio was in a Florida hospital recovering from pneumonia.

One of Yankee Stadium's most popular attractions: the Monument Park in center field..

LET'S GO

STADIUM
1950
1951
1952
1953
1956
1958
1961
1962
1977
1978
1996
GATE 4
ENTRY

New York Metropolitan Opera star Robert Merrill sang the National Anthem before Game Two.

The Roger Maris family threw out the ceremonial first pitch before Game Two.

"Buy me some peanuts and . . ."

Twenty-four year old Derek Jeter sits between two baseball veterans: Don Zimmer (left), who celebrated his 50th year in Major League Baseball in 1998, and Joe Torre, one of five who have managed and played in more than 2,000 major league games.

World Series
1998

Getty
MetLife
Armitron
7:50
OFFICIAL TIME
PADRES
YANKEES
HITACHI
ULTRAVISI
A TOTALLY NEW
BALL STRIKE OUT
0 0 0
Delta Air Lines
XEROX

The Yankee Stadium grounds crew danced to "Y-M-C-A."

NYPD
NYPD
N.Y.C.
POLICE
NYPD
PADRES
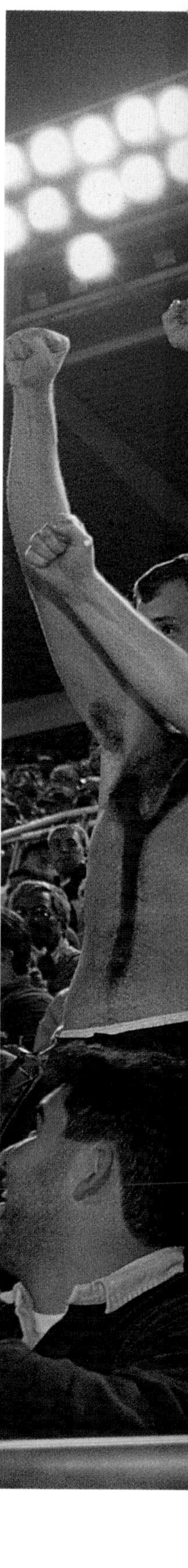

THE FALL Classic

Denzel Washington (left) and Bruce Willis (right) were part of the Game One crowd.

FOX-TV stars Luke Perry (left) and Calista Flockhart (center).

Tony Bennett performed the National Anthem before Game One.

Chris Rock attended Game Two.

DEER PARK
Budweiser
318 FT.
Kodak

Getty
Value Leader In Gasolines
MetLife
adidas
NATIONAL LEAGUE
399 FT.

Fans didn't forget Yankees outfielder Darryl Strawberry, who was recovering from cancer surgery.

NY AT BAT BALL STRIKE OUT INN
9 0 0 9

Jimmy D'Angelo, a 14-year-old who suffered serious injuries when struck by a foul ball at Yankee Stadium, was invited by Yankees Owner George Steinbrenner to occasionally work as a bat boy. The Yankees won all seven games young D'Angelo worked—including Game Four of the World Series.

BEING THERE

UP WITH SAN DIEGO!

Mark Whicker

There are roughly 1.45 million things to do in San Diego besides taking in a baseball game, and for most of 30 years, San Diegans have done them.

The Major League Padres were born in 1969 and triggered a frenzy of civic indifference. Not once in their first five seasons did they draw as many as 650,000 fans — and, yes, they had a new stadium. The problem was that the Triple-A Padres of the Pacific Coast League played in the same ballpark in 1968, and some of the same suspects were now expansion major leaguers.

"They were asking fans to see (minor leaguers) at higher prices,'' said a lifelong Padres employee. "That was not going to work."

It got better. And in 1998, the Padres won 98 games and the National League pennant and eventually persuaded the populace to build a new downtown ballpark. Well into the Tony Gwynn era, their top celebrities were The San Diego Chicken, oft-imitated mascot, and broadcaster Jerry Coleman, the ex-Yankee and a decorated Marine pilot in World War II. In the booth, he flies malaprops, such as, "He slid into second with a stand-up double.''

The Padres have never thrown a no-hitter, although manager Preston Gomez pinch-hit for Clay Kirby in 1970 when Kirby was losing a 1-0 no-hitter to the Mets. (San Diego lost 3-0, and the pinch-hitter was Cito Gaston, later a two-time world champion manager in Toronto.)

Until they won the 1984 NL pennant, they never finished above fourth. They traded Ozzie Smith and Robby Alomar, and lost Dave Winfield to free agency. "My first spring training, they fired (manager) Alvin Dark before we even got to Opening Day,'' Ozzie Smith said. "San Diego was a great place to play, but there came time to go other places and win. A lot of us grew up there.''

In the middle of the 1973 season the Padres were told they were moving to Washington. But when John Witt, the San Diego city attorney, told the new owners they were liable for the rest of the Padres' 30-year lease, the deal collapsed. That's why franchises don't skip their leases today. But until Gwynn came along with his eight batting championships, and until the Padres came back from 0-2 to upset the Cubs in the 1984 NL Championship Series, that was San Diego's contribution to baseball stability.

The Padres again seemed doomed in 1993. Tom Werner, producer of *The Cosby Show*, bought the team when the owners convinced him their plans would work, and that salaries would be controlled. When salaries skyrocketed, the Padres had to unload Gary Sheffield and Fred McGriff, and there were reports he would trade Heathcliff Huxtable for Heathcliff Slocumb.

"Things looked bleak,'' Gwynn recalled. "But when I heard we

got (reliever) Trevor Hoffman for Sheffield, I thought, well, it's not all bad."

During the 1994 players' strike, John Moores bought the club from Werner. Moores got rich off computers but also enjoyed giving money away, to players and community projects. His belief in winning put the Padres back on track. And, as the l998 Series ended, he awaited the results of an initiative for a new ballpark in San Diego. He got it.

"In New York, tradition is Ruth and Gehrig and DiMaggio," said Graig Nettles, a San Diego native who played for the Yankees and Padres. It had been not quite the same in San Diego, he allowed.

Nonetheless, baseball actually runs thick in San Diego's blood.

Don Larsen and David Wells, who pitched perfect games for the Yankees 32 years apart, are San Diegans. And Ted Williams hailed from Hoover High. He signed with the Pacific Coast League Padres in 1936, when owner Bill Lane moved the Hollywood Stars to San Diego and built Lane Stadium downtown. Williams used to drive foul balls into the Pacific. He also hit .291 in 1937 with 23 home runs.

Jack Graham might have swatted 60 in 1948, but was beaned by Red Adams of the Los Angeles Angels on July 27, in a series his manager, Rip Collins, advised him to sit out. An old scout named Jack Hughes used to tell everyone, "Only Southern California Edison has more power than Jack Graham."

Max West followed up with 48 homers in l949. Later, a groundskeeper discovered why — it was only 325 feet from home plate to the right field wall, and, for that matter, 87 feet down the first base line.

San Diego can't give us championship stories the way the Yankees can, but it can sit us down and talk about Gwynn, Gaylord Perry, Randy Jones and Goose Gossage. It takes its losses hard — all the way into the parking lot. Game Three of 1998 World Series hurt quite a bit, especially when the Padres got a man to third base in the ninth and left him there, losing 5-4.

"We're going to the bottom of the wire!" Jerry Coleman proclaimed. In San Diego they smile, whether their hearts are breaking or not.

Mark Whicker is a sports columnist for *The Orange County Register.*

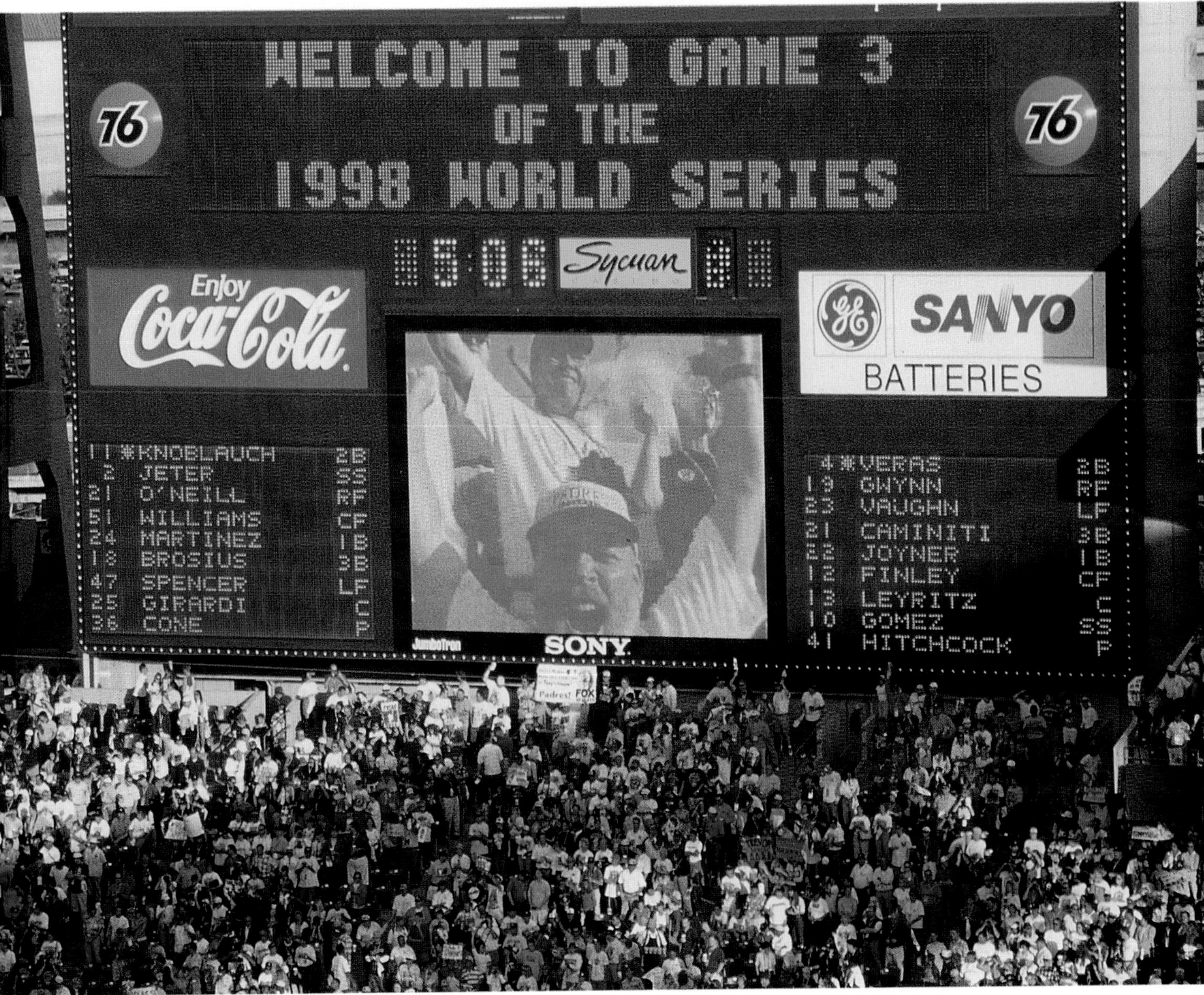
WELCOME TO GAME 3
OF THE
1998 WORLD SERIES
76
76
5:06
Sycuan
Enjoy
Coca-Cola
SANYO
BATTERIES
11 *KNOBLAUCH 2B
2 JETER SS
21 O'NEILL RF
51 WILLIAMS CF
24 MARTINEZ 1B
18 BROSIUS 3B
47 SPENCER LF
25 GIRARDI C
36 CONE P
4 *VERAS 2B
19 GWYNN RF
23 VAUGHN LF
21 CAMINITI 3B
22 JOYNER 1B
12 FINLEY CF
13 LEYRITZ C
10 GOMEZ SS
41 HITCHCOCK P
JumboTron
SONY
Padres!

POSTALANNEX
51

JETER
2
KFMB
COX

1998

DAMN
YANKEES

Office DEPOT
WELCOME TO THE
1998 WORLD SERIES
BUD LIGHT
QUALCOMM
Konica
YES ON C
GAP

TOYOTA

PADRES

LEAGUE
CHAMPIONS
SAN DIEGO
PADRES

Managers Joe Torre and Bruce Bochy met with the umpires to discuss the ground rules before Game Three.

Mr. October, Reggie Jackson.

Only in San Diego would Paul O'Neill retrieve a beach ball from the stands.

Buffy the Vampire Slayer *Sarah Michelle Gellar with Andrew Shue.*

The producer of A League of Their Own, *Penny Marshall.*

It's Garry Shandling.

Three San Diego Amigos and a die-hard Padres fan.

IT'S
TREVOR
TIME!
Union-Tribune.

FOR THE RECORD

Game One

San Diego Padres @ New York Yankees, 10/17/1998

San Diego Padres	AB	R	H	RBI	BB	SO
Veras 2b	4	1	1	0	1	0
Gwynn rf	4	1	3	2	0	0
Vaughn lf	4	3	2	3	0	0
Caminiti 3b	3	0	0	0	1	2
Leyritz dh	4	0	0	0	0	2
Joyner 1b	3	0	0	0	1	1
Finley cf	4	0	1	0	0	0
Hernandez c	3	0	0	0	0	0
G. Myers ph	1	0	0	0	0	1
Gomez ss	3	1	1	0	0	0
Vander Wal ph	1	0	0	0	0	1
Brown p	0	0	0	0	0	0
Wall p	0	0	0	0	0	0
Langston p	0	0	0	0	0	0
Boehringer p	0	0	0	0	0	0
R. Myers p	0	0	0	0	0	0
TOTALS	**34**	**6**	**8**	**5**	**3**	**7**

New York Yankees	AB	R	H	RBI	BB	SO
Knoblauch 2b	4	1	2	3	0	1
Jeter ss	4	1	1	0	1	0
O'Neill rf	5	0	0	0	0	1
Williams cf	4	1	0	0	1	3
Davis dh	3	2	1	0	1	0
Martinez 1b	3	2	1	4	1	1
Brosius 3b	4	0	1	0	0	1
Posada c	3	1	1	0	1	1
Ledee lf	3	1	2	2	1	0
Wells p	0	0	0	0	0	0
Nelson p	0	0	0	0	0	0
Rivera p	0	0	0	0	0	0
TOTALS	**33**	**9**	**9**	**9**	**6**	**8**

San Diego	0 0 2	0 3 0	0 1 0 -	6 8 1
New York	0 2 0	0 0 0	7 0 x -	9 9 1

E-Vaughn, Knoblauch. DP-New York 2. LOB-San Diego 4, New York 7.

2B-Finley, Ledee. HR-Gwynn, Vaughn 2, Knoblauch, Martinez.

San Diego Padres		INN	H	R	ER	BB	SO
Brown		6.1	6	4	4	3	5
Wall	L	0.0	2	2	2	0	0
Langston		0.2	1	3	3	2	0
Boehringer		0.1	0	0	0	1	1
R. Myers		0.2	0	0	0	0	2
TOTALS		**8.0**	**9**	**9**	**9**	**6**	**8**

New York Yankees		INN	H	R	ER	BB	SO
Wells	W	7.0	7	5	5	2	4
Nelson		0.2	1	1	0	1	1
Rivera	SV	1.1	0	0	0	0	2
TOTALS		**9.0**	**8**	**6**	**5**	**3**	**7**

Wall pitched to 2 batters in the 7th. WP-Langston. HBP-Boehringer (Knoblauch). T-3:29. A-56,712. Umpires-HP, Garcia; 1B, M. Hirschbeck; 2B, Scott; 3B, DeMuth; LF, Tschida; RF, Crawford.

Game 1
HOW THE RUNS WERE SCORED

Yankees 2nd- Williams grounded out: Caminiti to Joyner. Davis singled to the pitcher. Martinez walked. Brosius struck out swinging. Posada walked. Ledee doubled to right, Davis scored, Martinez scored, Posada advanced to third. Knoblauch struck out swinging. (2 Runs, 2 Hits, 0 Errors, 2 LOB)
Padres 3rd- Gomez singled to left. Veras flied out to O'Neill. Gwynn grounded out to Martinez, Gomez advanced to second. Vaughn homered to right on an 0-2 count, Gomez scored. Caminiti struck out swinging. (2 Runs, 2 Hits, 0 Errors, 0 LOB)
Padres 5th- Hernandez flied out to Ledee. Gomez popped out to Jeter. Veras singled to center. Gwynn homered to right on a 0-0 count, Veras scored. Vaughn homered to left on a 0-0 count. Caminiti flied out to Ledee. (3 Runs, 3 Hits, 0 Errors, 0 LOB)
Yankees 7th-Brosius grounded out: Veras to Joyner. Posada singled to right. Ledee walked. Wall came in to pitch for the Padres. Knoblauch homered to left on a 2-0 count, Posada scored, Ledee scored. Jeter singled to center. Langston came in to pitch for the Padres. O'Neill flied out to Gwynn. With Williams batting, Jeter advanced to second on Langston's wild pitch. Williams was walked intentionally. Davis walked. Martinez homered to right on a 3-2 count, Jeter scored, Williams scored, Davis scored. Brosius flied out to Finley. (7 Runs, 4 Hits, 0 Errors, 0 LOB)
Padres 8th- Nelson came in to pitch for the Yankees. Gwynn singled to right. Vaughn reached first on the fielder's choice, Gwynn out: Nelson to Knoblauch. Caminiti walked. Leyritz struck out swinging. Rivera came in to pitch for the Yankees. Joyner reached first on Knoblauch's error, Vaughn scored on the error, Caminiti advanced to second on the error. Finley grounded out to Martinez. (1 Run, 1 Hit, 1 Error, 2 LOB)

Game Two

San Diego Padres @ New York Yankees, 10/18/1998

San Diego Padres	AB	R	H	RBI	BB	SO
Veras 2b	5	0	1	1	0	3
Gwynn rf	4	0	1	0	1	0
Vaughn dh	4	0	0	0	1	1
Caminiti 3b	5	1	1	0	0	2
Joyner 1b	2	0	0	0	1	0
Leyritz ph-1b	1	0	0	0	0	1
Finley cf	4	0	0	0	0	1
Vander Wal lf	3	0	2	0	0	1
Rivera ph-lf	1	1	1	1	0	0
G. Myers c	3	0	0	0	0	1
Hernandez ph-c	1	0	1	0	0	0
Gomez ss	3	1	2	0	0	0
Sweeney ph	1	0	1	1	0	0
Sheets ss	0	0	0	0	0	0
Ashby p	0	0	0	0	0	0
Boehringer p	0	0	0	0	0	0
Wall p	0	0	0	0	0	0
Miceli p	0	0	0	0	0	0
TOTALS	**37**	**3**	**10**	**3**	**3**	**10**

New York Yankees	AB	R	H	RBI	BB	SO
Knoblauch 2b	3	2	2	0	2	1
Jeter ss	5	1	2	1	0	1
O'Neill rf	5	1	1	0	0	0
Williams cf	4	1	1	2	1	0
Davis dh	3	1	1	1	2	2
Bush pr-dh	0	0	0	0	0	0
Martinez 1b	5	1	3	0	0	0
Brosius 3b	5	1	3	1	0	1
Posada c	4	1	1	2	1	0
Ledee lf	3	0	2	1	1	0
Hernandez p	0	0	0	0	0	0

New York Yankees	AB	R	H	RBI	BB	SO
Stanton p	0	0	0	0	0	0
Nelson p	0	0	0	0	0	0
TOTALS	**37**	**9**	**16**	**8**	**7**	**5**

San Diego	0 0 0	0 1 0	0 2 0 -	3 10 1
New York	3 3 1	0 2 0	0 0 x -	9 16 0

E-Caminiti. DP-San Diego 3. LOB-San Diego 10, New York (A.L.) 11. 2B-Veras, Caminiti, Vander Wal, Rivera, Ledee. 3B-Gomez. HR-Williams, Posada. SB-Knoblauch.

San Diego Padres		INN	H	R	ER	BB	SO
Ashby	L	2.2	10	7	4	1	1
Boehringer		1.2	4	2	2	1	2
Wall		2.2	1	0	0	3	1
Miceli		1.0	1	0	0	2	1
TOTALS		**8.0**	**16**	**9**	**6**	**7**	**5**

New York Yankees		INN	H	R	ER	BB	SO
Hernandez	W	7.0	6	1	1	3	7
Stanton		0.2	3	2	2	0	1
Nelson		1.1	1	0	0	0	2
TOTALS		**9.0**	**10**	**3**	**3**	**3**	**10**

T-3:31. A-56,692. Umpires-HP, M. Hirschbeck; 1B, Scott; 2B, DeMuth; 3B,Tschida; LF, Crawford; RF, Garcia.

Game 2
HOW THE RUNS WERE SCORED

Yankees 1st- Knoblauch walked. With Jeter batting, Knoblauch stole second. Jeter grounded out: Ashby to Joyner. O'Neill reached first on Caminiti's error, Knoblauch scored on the error. Williams grounded out: Ashby to Joyner, O'Neill advanced to second. Davis singled to center, O'Neill scored. Martinez singled to right, Davis advanced to third. Brosius singled to left, Davis scored, Martinez advanced to second. Posada grounded out: Veras to Joyner. (3 Runs, 3 Hits, 1 Error, 2 LOB)
Yankees 2nd- Ledee singled to right. Knoblauch singled to third, Ledee advanced to second. With Jeter batting, Ledee caught stealing: G. Myers to Caminiti, Knoblauch advanced to second. Jeter singled to center, Knoblauch scored. O'Neill flied out to Vander Wal. Williams homered to right on a 3-2 count, Jeter scored. Davis struck out swinging. (3 Runs, 4 Hits, 0 Errors, 0 LOB)
Yankees 3rd- Martinez singled to center. Brosius singled to left, Martinez advanced to second. Posada grounded into a double play, Martinez advanced to third, Brosius out: Veras to Gomez to Joyner. Ledee doubled to left, Martinez scored. Boehringer came in to pitch for the Padres. Knoblauch struck out looking. (1 Run, 3 Hits, 0 Errors, 1 LOB)
Padres 5th- Vander Wal struck out looking. G. Myers struck out swinging. Gomez tripled to right. Veras doubled to right, Gomez scored. Gwynn grounded out: Hernandez to Martinez. (1 Run, 2 Hits, 0 Errors, 1 LOB)
Yankees 5th- Martinez popped out to Caminiti. Brosius singled to left. Posada homered to right on a 1-2 count, Brosius scored. Ledee walked. Knoblauch singled to right, Ledee advanced to second. Wall came in to pitch for the Padres. Jeter struck out swinging. O'Neill grounded out: Veras to Joyner. (2 Runs, 3 Hits, 0 Errors, 2 LOB)
Padres 8th- Stanton came in to pitch for the Yankees. Caminiti doubled to left. Leyritz pinch hit for Joyner. Leyritz struck out swinging. Finley grounded out: Knoblauch to Martinez, Caminiti advanced to third. Rivera pinch hit for Vander Wal. Rivera doubled to left, Caminiti scored. Hernandez pinch hit for G. Myers. Hernandez singled to second, Rivera advanced to third. Nelson came in to pitch for the Yankees. Sweeney pinch hit for Gomez. Sweeney singled to right, Rivera scored, Hernandez advanced to second. Veras struck out swinging. (2 Runs, 4 Hits, 0 Errors, 2 LOB)

Game Three
New York Yankees @ San Diego Padres, 10/20/1998

New York Yankees	AB	R	H	RBI	BB	SO
Knoblauch 2b	4	0	1	0	1	0
Jeter ss	4	0	1	0	1	1
O'Neill rf	4	1	1	0	1	1
Williams cf	4	0	0	0	0	2
Martinez 1b	3	1	0	0	1	0
Brosius 3b	4	2	3	4	0	0
Spencer lf	3	1	1	0	0	2
Ledee ph-lf	1	0	0	0	0	0
Girardi c	2	0	0	0	0	1
Posada ph-c	2	0	1	0	0	1
Cone p	2	0	1	0	0	0
Davis ph	1	0	0	1	0	0
Bush pr	0	0	0	0	0	0
Lloyd p	0	0	0	0	0	0
Mendoza p	1	0	0	0	0	0
Rivera p	0	0	0	0	0	0
TOTALS	**35**	**5**	**9**	**5**	**4**	**8**

San Diego Padres	AB	R	H	RBI	BB	SO
Veras 2b	3	2	1	0	1	0
Gwynn rf	4	1	2	1	0	0
Rivera pr-rf	0	0	0	0	0	0
Vaughn lf	3	0	0	1	0	0
Caminiti 3b	2	0	0	1	1	2
Joyner 1b	3	0	0	0	1	0
Finley cf	4	0	0	0	0	1
Leyritz c	2	0	0	0	0	1
Hernandez c	2	0	1	0	0	1
Vander Wal pr	0	0	0	0	0	0
Gomez ss	3	0	1	0	0	1
Hoffman p	0	0	0	0	0	0
Sweeney ph	1	0	1	0	0	0
Hitchcock p	2	1	1	0	0	0
Hamilton p	0	0	0	0	0	0
R. Myers p	0	0	0	0	0	0
Sheets ss	2	0	0	0	0	1
TOTALS	**31**	**4**	**7**	**3**	**3**	**7**

New York	0 0 0	0 0 0	2 3 0 -	5 9 1
San Diego	0 0 0	0 0 3	0 1 0 -	4 7 1

E-O'Neill, Caminiti. DP-San Diego 2. LOB-New York 7, San Diego 5. 2B-Spencer, Veras. HR-Brosius 2. SB-Finley. SF-Vaughn, Caminiti.

New York Yankees		INN	H	R	ER	BB	SO
Cone		6.0	2	3	2	3	4
Lloyd		0.1	0	0	0	0	0
Mendoza	W	1.0	2	1	1	0	1
Rivera	SV	1.2	3	0	0	0	2
TOTALS		**9.0**	**7**	**4**	**3**	**3**	**7**

San Diego Padres		INN	H	R	ER	BB	SO
Hitchcock		6.0	7	2	1	1	7
Hamilton		1.0	0	0	0	1	1
R. Myers		0.0	0	1	1	1	0
Hoffman	L	2.0	2	2	2	1	0
TOTALS		**9.0**	**9**	**5**	**4**	**4**	**8**

Hitchcock pitched to 2 batters in the 7th. R. Myers pitched to 1 batter in the 8th. T-3:14. A-64,667. Umpires-HP, Scott; 1B, DeMuth; 2B, Tschida; 3B, Crawford; LF, Garcia; RF, M. Hirschbeck. OS-Foley, Street, Collier.

Game 3
HOW THE RUNS WERE SCORED

Padres 6th- Hitchcock singled to right. Veras walked. Gwynn singled to right, advanced to third on O'Neill's error, Hitchcock scored, Veras scored on the error. Vaughn grounded out: Jeter to Martinez. Caminiti hit a sacrifice fly to Williams, Gwynn scored. Joyner grounded out: Martinez to Cone. (3 Runs, 2 Hits, 1 Error, 0 LOB)
Yankees 7th- Brosius homered to left on a 3-2 count. Spencer doubled to left Hamilton came in to pitch for the Padres, batting 9th. Posada pinch hit for Girardi. With Posada batting, Spencer advanced to third: Leyritz (PB). Posada struck out swinging. Davis pinch hit for Cone. Davis reached first on Caminiti's error, Spencer scored. Bush ran for Davis. Hernandez went to catcher, batting 7th. Knoblauch walked. Jeter lined out, Bush out: Gomez to Veras (double play). (2 Runs, 2 Hits, 1 Error, 1 LOB)
Yankees 8th-R. Myers came in to pitch for the Padres, batting 9th. O'Neill walked. Sheets went to short, batting 9th. Hoffman came in to pitch for the Padres, batting 8th. Williams flied out to Gwynn. Martinez walked. Brosius homered to center on a 2-2 count, O'Neill scored, Martinez scored. Ledee pinch hit for Spencer. Ledee grounded out: Veras to Joyner. Posada singled to center. Mendoza grounded out: Sheets to Joyner. (3 Runs, 2 Hits, 0 Errors, 1 LOB)
Padres 8th- Ledee went to left field. Sheets grounded out: Brosius to Martinez. Veras doubled to left. Rivera came in to pitch for the Yankees, batting 9th. Gwynn singled to left, Veras advanced to third. Rivera ran for Gwynn. Vaughn hit a sacrifice fly to O'Neill, Veras scored. Caminiti struck out swinging. (1 Run, 2 Hits, 0 Errors, 1 LOB)

Game Four
New York Yankees @ San Diego Padres, 10/21/1998

New York Yankees	AB	R	H	RBI	BB	SO
Knoblauch 2b	5	0	1	0	0	0
Jeter ss	4	2	2	0	1	1
O'Neill rf	5	1	2	0	0	0
Williams cf	4	0	0	1	0	0
Martinez 1b	2	0	1	0	2	1
Brosius 3b	4	0	1	1	0	2
Ledee lf	3	0	2	1	0	1
Girardi c	4	0	0	0	0	1
Pettitte p	2	0	0	0	0	2
Nelson p	0	0	0	0	0	0
Rivera p	1	0	0	0	0	0
TOTALS	**34**	**3**	**9**	**3**	**3**	**8**

San Diego Padres	AB	R	H	RBI	BB	SO
Veras 2b	3	0	0	0	1	1
Gwynn rf	4	0	2	0	0	0
Vaughn lf	4	0	0	0	0	1
Caminiti 3b	4	0	1	0	0	1
Leyritz 1b	3	0	0	0	1	0
Rivera cf	4	0	3	0	0	0
Hernandez c	4	0	0	0	0	2
Gomez ss	2	0	0	0	1	0
Sweeney ph	1	0	0	0	0	0
Brown p	2	0	1	0	0	0
Vander Wal ph	1	0	0	0	0	0
Miceli p	0	0	0	0	0	0
R. Myers p	0	0	0	0	0	0
TOTALS	**32**	**0**	**7**	**0**	**3**	**5**

New York	0 0 0	0 0 1	0 2 0 -	3 9 0
San Diego	0 0 0	0 0 0	0 0 0 -	0 7 0

DP-New York 2. LOB-New York 9, San Diego 8. 2B-O'Neill, Ledee, Rivera. SH-Pettitte. SF-Ledee.

New York Yankees		INN	H	R	ER	BB	SO
Pettitte	W	7.1	5	0	0	3	4
Nelson		0.1	0	0	0	0	1
Rivera	SV	1.1	2	0	0	0	0
TOTALS		**9.0**	**7**	**0**	**0**	**3**	**5**

San Diego Padres		INN	H	R	ER	BB	SO
Brown	L	8.0	8	3	3	3	8
Miceli		0.2	1	0	0	0	0
R. Myers		0.1	0	0	0	0	0
TOTALS		**9.0**	**9**	**3**	**3**	**3**	**8**

T-2:58. A-65,427. Umpires-HP, DeMuth; 1B, Tschida; 2B, Crawford; 3B, Garcia; LF, M. Hirschbeck; RF, Scott.

Game 4
HOW THE RUNS WERE SCORED

Yankees 6th- Knoblauch grounded out: Veras to Leyritz. Jeter singled to short. O'Neill doubled to right, Jeter advanced to third. Williams grounded out: Brown to Leyritz, Jeter scored, O'Neill advanced to third. Martinez was walked intentionally. Brosius struck out swinging. (1 Run, 2 Hits, 0 Errors, 2 LOB)
Yankees 8th- Jeter walked. O'Neill singled to first, Jeter advanced to second. Williams grounded out: Caminiti to Leyritz, Jeter advanced to third, O'Neill advanced to second. Martinez was walked intentionally. Brosius singled to left, Jeter scored, O'Neill advanced to third, Martinez advanced to second. Ledee hit a sacrifice fly to Vaughn, O'Neill scored. Girardi grounded out: Veras to Leyritz. (2 Runs, 2 Hits, 0 Errors, 2 LOB)

NEW YORK YANKEES

Batting

NAME	Avg.	G	AB	R	H	TB	2B	3B	HR	RBI	BB	SO	SB	CS	SLG	OBP	E
Brosius	.471	4	17	3	8	14	0	0	2	6	0	4	0	0	.824	.471	0
Bush	---	2	0	0	0	0	0	0	0	0	0	0	0	0	---	---	0
Cone	.500	1	2	0	1	1	0	0	0	0	0	0	0	0	.500	.500	0
Curtis	---	0	0	0	0	0	0	0	0	0	0	0	0	0	---	---	0
Davis	.286	3	7	3	2	2	0	0	0	2	3	2	0	0	.286	.500	0
Girardi	.000	2	6	0	0	0	0	0	0	0	0	2	0	0	.000	.000	0
Hernandez	---	1	0	0	0	0	0	0	0	0	0	0	0	0	---	---	0
Irabu	---	0	0	0	0	0	0	0	0	0	0	0	0	0	---	---	0
Jeter	.353	4	17	4	6	6	0	0	0	1	3	3	0	0	.353	.450	0
Knoblauch	.375	4	16	3	6	9	0	0	1	3	3	2	1	0	.563	.500	1
Ledee	.600	4	10	1	6	9	3	0	0	4	2	1	0	1	.900	.615	0
Lloyd	---	1	0	0	0	0	0	0	0	0	0	0	0	0	---	---	0
Martinez	.385	4	13	4	5	8	0	0	1	4	4	2	0	0	.615	.529	0
Mendoza	.000	1	1	0	0	0	0	0	0	0	0	0	0	0	.000	.000	0
Nelson	---	3	0	0	0	0	0	0	0	0	0	0	0	0	---	---	0
O'Neill	.211	4	19	3	4	5	1	0	0	0	1	2	0	0	.263	.250	1
Pettitte	.000	1	2	0	0	0	0	0	0	0	0	2	0	0	.000	.000	0
Posada	.333	3	9	2	3	6	0	0	1	2	2	2	0	0	.667	.455	0
Raines	---	0	0	0	0	0	0	0	0	0	0	0	0	0	---	---	0
Rivera	.000	3	1	0	0	0	0	0	0	0	0	0	0	0	.000	.000	0
Sojo	---	0	0	0	0	0	0	0	0	0	0	0	0	0	---	---	0
Spencer	.333	1	3	1	1	2	1	0	0	0	0	2	0	0	.667	.333	0
Stanton	---	1	0	0	0	0	0	0	0	0	0	0	0	0	---	---	0
Wells	---	1	0	0	0	0	0	0	0	0	0	0	0	0	---	---	0
Williams	.063	4	16	2	1	4	0	0	1	3	2	5	0	0	.250	.167	0
TEAM	**.309**	**4**	**139**	**26**	**43**	**66**	**5**	**0**	**6**	**25**	**20**	**29**	**1**	**1**	**.475**	**.398**	**2**

S-Pettitte SF-Ledee

Pitching

NAME	G	GS	Opp W	L	SV	ERA	BA	INN	H	R	ER	HR	BB	IBB	SO
Cone	1	1	0	0	0	3.00	.105	6.0	2	3	2	0	3	0	4
Hernandez	1	1	1	0	0	1.29	.222	7.0	6	1	1	0	3	0	7
Irabu	0	0	0	0	0	----	---	0	0	0	0	0	0	0	0
Lloyd	1	0	0	0	0	0.00	.000	0.1	0	0	0	0	0	0	0
Mendoza	1	0	1	0	0	9.00	.500	1.0	2	1	1	0	0	0	1
Nelson	3	0	0	0	0	0.00	.222	2.1	2	1	0	0	1	0	4
Pettitte	1	1	1	0	0	0.00	.192	7.1	5	0	0	0	3	0	4
Rivera	3	0	0	0	3	0.00	.294	4.1	5	0	0	0	0	0	4
Stanton	1	0	0	0	0	27.00	.600	0.2	3	2	2	0	0	0	1
Wells	1	1	1	0	0	6.43	.269	7.0	7	5	5	3	2	0	4
TEAM	**4**	**4**	**4**	**0**	**3**	**2.75**	**.239**	**36.0**	**32**	**13**	**11**	**3**	**12**	**0**	**29**

SAN DIEGO PADRES

Batting

NAME	Avg.	G	AB	R	H	TB	2B	3B	HR	RBI	BB	SO	SB	CS	SLG	OBP	E
Arias	---	0	0	0	0	0	0	0	0	0	0	0	0	0	---	---	0
Ashby	---	1	0	0	0	0	0	0	0	0	0	0	0	0	---	---	0
Boehringer	---	2	0	0	0	0	0	0	0	0	0	0	0	0	---	---	0
Brown	.500	2	2	0	1	1	0	0	0	0	0	0	0	0	.500	.500	0
Caminiti	.143	4	14	1	2	3	1	0	0	1	2	7	0	0	.214	.235	2
Finley	.083	3	12	0	1	2	1	0	0	0	0	2	1	0	.167	.083	0
Gomez	.364	4	11	2	4	6	0	1	0	0	1	1	0	0	.545	.417	0
Gwynn	.500	4	16	2	8	11	0	0	1	3	1	0	0	0	.688	.529	0
Hamilton	---	1	0	0	0	0	0	0	0	0	0	0	0	0	---	---	0
Hernandez	.200	4	10	0	2	2	0	0	0	0	0	3	0	0	.200	.200	0
Hitchcock	.500	1	2	1	1	1	0	0	0	0	0	0	0	0	.500	.500	0
Hoffman	---	1	0	0	0	0	0	0	0	0	0	0	0	0	---	---	0
Joyner	.000	3	8	0	0	0	0	0	0	0	3	1	0	0	.000	.273	0
Langston	---	1	0	0	0	0	0	0	0	0	0	0	0	0	---	---	0
Leyritz	.000	4	1	0	0	0	0	0	0	0	1	4	0	0	.000	.091	0
Miceli	---	2	0	0	0	0	0	0	0	0	0	0	0	0	---	---	0
G. Myers	.000	2	4	0	0	0	0	0	0	0	0	2	0	0	.000	.000	0
R. Myers	---	3	0	0	0	0	0	0	0	0	0	0	0	0	---	---	0
Rivera	.800	3	5	1	4	6	2	0	0	1	0	0	0	0	1.200	.800	0
Sheets	.000	2	2	0	0	0	0	0	0	0	0	1	0	0	.000	.000	0
Sweeney	.667	3	3	0	2	2	0	0	0	1	0	0	0	0	.667	.667	0
Vander Wal	.400	4	5	0	2	3	1	0	0	0	0	2	0	0	.600	.400	0
Vaughn	.133	4	15	3	2	8	0	0	2	4	1	2	0	0	.533	.176	1
Veras	.200	4	15	3	3	5	2	0	0	1	3	4	0	0	.333	.333	0
Wall	---	2	0	0	0	0	0	0	0	0	0	0	0	0	---	---	0
TEAM	**.239**	**4**	**134**	**13**	**32**	**50**	**7**	**1**	**3**	**11**	**12**	**29**	**1**	**0**	**.373**	**.297**	**3**

SF-Caminiti, Vaughn

Pitching

NAME	G	GS	Opp W	L	S	ERA	BA	INN	H	R	ER	HR	BB	IBB	SO
Ashby	1	1	0	1	0	13.50	.588	2.2	10	7	4	1	1	0	1
Boehringer	2	0	0	0	0	9.00	.364	2.0	4	2	2	1	2	0	3
Brown	2	2	0	1	0	4.40	.259	14.1	14	7	7	0	6	2	13
Hamilton	1	0	0	0	0	0.00	.000	1.0	0	0	0	0	1	0	1
Hitchcock	1	1	0	0	0	1.50	.292	6.0	7	2	1	1	1	0	7
Hoffman	1	0	0	1	0	9.00	.250	2.0	2	2	2	1	1	0	0
Langston	1	0	0	0	0	40.50	.333	0.2	1	3	3	1	2	1	0
Miceli	2	0	0	0	0	0.00	.286	1.2	2	0	0	0	2	0	1
R. Myers	3	0	0	0	0	9.00	.000	1.0	0	1	1	0	1	0	2
Wall	2	0	0	1	0	6.75	.333	2.2	3	2	2	1	3	0	1
TEAM	**4**	**4**	**0**	**4**	**0**	**5.82**	**.309**	**34.0**	**43**	**26**	**22**	**6**	**20**	**3**	**29**

WP-Langston HB-Boehringer

Significant Records Set and Tied During the 1998 World Series

Researched by the Elias Sports Bureau, Inc.

GENERAL CLUB RECORDS SET

Most World Series:
35, New York Yankees

Most World Series Won:
24, New York Yankees

Most World Series Games:
197, New York Yankees

Most World Series Games Won:
117, New York Yankees

Most Players, Both Clubs, 4-Game Series:
45, San Diego Padres (24) and New York Yankees (21)

Most Pitchers, 4-Game Series:
10, San Diego Padres

Most Pitchers, Both Clubs, 4-Game Series:
19, San Diego Padres (10) and New York Yankees (9)

CLUB BATTING RECORDS SET

Most Singles, 4-Game Series:
32, New York Yankees

CLUB BATTING RECORDS TIED

Most Home Runs, Consecutive, Inning:
2, San Diego Padres, Oct. 17 (Game One)

Fewest Triples, Both Clubs, 4-Game Series:
1, New York Yankees (0) and San Diego Padres (1)

Most Sacrifice Flies, 4-Game Series:
2, San Diego Padres

Most Sacrifice Flies, Both Clubs, 4-Game Series:
3, New York Yankees (1) and San Diego Padres (2)

CLUB PITCHING RECORDS SET

Most Saves, 4-Game Series:
3, New York Yankees

INDIVIDUAL BATTING RECORDS TIED

Most Home Runs, First Game (of career):
2, Greg Vaughn, S.D.

Most Home Runs, Consecutive Innings:
2, Scott Brosius, N.Y., Oct. 20 (Game Three)

Most At-Bats, 4-Game Series:
19, Paul O'Neill, N.Y.

Most Intentional Walks, 4-Game Series:
2, Tino Martinez, N.Y.

Most Strikeouts, 4-Game Series:
7, Ken Caminiti, S.D.

INDIVIDUAL PITCHING RECORDS SET

Most Saves, 4-Game Series:
3, Mariano Rivera, N.Y.

INDIVIDUAL PITCHING RECORDS TIED

Most Games Finished, 4-Games Series:
3, Mariano Rivera, N.Y.

Most Intentional Walks, 4-Game Series:
2, Kevin Brown, S.D.

All-Time World Series Winners and Losers

Year	Winner	LG	Loser	LG	Result
1903	Boston Pilgrims	AL	Pittsburgh Pirates	NL	5 - 3
1904	No Series				
1905	New York Giants	NL	Philadelphia Athletics	AL	4 - 1
1906	Chicago White Sox	AL	Chicago Cubs	NL	4 - 2
1907	Chicago Cubs	NL	Detroit Tigers	AL	4 - 0
1908	Chicago Cubs	NL	Detroit Tigers	AL	4 - 1
1909	Pittsburgh Pirates	NL	Detroit Tigers	AL	4 - 3
1910	Philadelphia Athletics	AL	Chicago Cubs	NL	4 - 1
1911	Philadelphia Athletics	AL	New York Giants	NL	4 - 2
1912	Boston Red Sox	AL	New York Giants	NL	4 - 3
1913	Philadelphia Athletics	AL	New York Giants	NL	4 - 1
1914	Boston Braves	NL	Philadelphia Athletics	AL	4 - 0
1915	Boston Red Sox	AL	Philadelphia Phillies	NL	4 - 1
1916	Boston Red Sox	AL	Brooklyn Dodgers	NL	4 - 1
1917	Chicago White Sox	AL	New York Giants	NL	4 - 2
1918	Boston Red Sox	AL	Chicago Cubs	NL	4 - 2
1919	Cincinnati Reds	NL	Chicago White Sox	AL	5 - 3
1920	Cleveland Indians	AL	Brooklyn Dodgers	NL	5 - 2
1921	New York Giants	NL	New York Yankees	AL	5 - 3
1922	New York Giants	NL	New York Yankees	AL	4 - 0
1923	New York Yankees	AL	New York Giants	NL	4 - 2
1924	Washington Senators	AL	New York Giants	NL	4 - 3
1925	Pittsburgh Pirates	NL	Washington Senators	AL	4 - 3
1926	St. Louis Cardinals	NL	New York Yankees	AL	4 - 3
1927	New York Yankees	AL	Pittsburgh Pirates	NL	4 - 0
1928	New York Yankees	AL	St. Louis Cardinals	NL	4 - 0
1929	Philadelphia Athletics	AL	Chicago Cubs	NL	4 - 1
1930	Philadelphia Athletics	AL	St. Louis Cardinals	NL	4 - 2
1931	St. Louis Cardinals	NL	Philadelphia Athletics	AL	4 - 3
1932	New York Yankees	AL	Chicago Cubs	NL	4 - 0
1933	New York Giants	NL	Washington Senators	AL	4 - 1
1934	St. Louis Cardinals	NL	Detroit Tigers	AL	4 - 3
1935	Detroit Tigers	AL	Chicago Cubs	NL	4 - 2
1936	New York Yankees	AL	New York Giants	NL	4 - 2
1937	New York Yankees	AL	New York Giants	NL	4 - 1
1938	New York Yankees	AL	Chicago Cubs	NL	4 - 0
1939	New York Yankees	AL	Cincinnati Reds	NL	4 - 0
1940	Cincinnati Reds	NL	Detroit Tigers	AL	4 - 3
1941	New York Yankees	AL	Brooklyn Dodgers	NL	4 - 1
1942	St. Louis Cardinals	NL	New York Yankees	AL	4 - 1
1943	New York Yankees	AL	St. Louis Cardinals	NL	4 - 1
1944	St. Louis Cardinals	NL	St. Louis Browns	AL	4 - 2
1945	Detroit Tigers	AL	Chicago Cubs	NL	4 - 3
1946	St. Louis Cardinals	NL	Boston Red Sox	AL	4 - 3
1947	New York Yankees	AL	Brooklyn Dodgers	NL	4 - 3
1948	Cleveland Indians	AL	Boston Braves	NL	4 - 2
1949	New York Yankees	AL	Brooklyn Dodgers	NL	4 - 1
1950	New York Yankees	AL	Philadelphia Phillies	NL	4 - 0
1951	New York Yankees	AL	New York Giants	NL	4 - 2
1952	New York Yankees	AL	Brooklyn Dodgers	NL	4 - 3
1953	New York Yankees	AL	Brooklyn Dodgers	NL	4 - 2
1954	New York Giants	NL	Cleveland Indians	AL	4 - 0
1955	Brooklyn Dodgers	NL	New York Yankees	AL	4 - 3
1956	New York Yankees	AL	Brooklyn Dodgers	NL	4 - 3
1957	Milwaukee Braves	NL	New York Yankees	AL	4 - 3
1958	New York Yankees	AL	Milwaukee Braves	NL	4 - 3
1959	Los Angeles Dodgers	NL	Chicago White Sox	AL	4 - 2
1960	Pittsburgh Pirates	NL	New York Yankees	AL	4 - 3
1961	New York Yankees	AL	Cincinnati Reds	NL	4 - 1
1962	New York Yankees	AL	San Francisco Giants	NL	4 - 3
1963	Los Angeles Dodgers	NL	New York Yankees	AL	4 - 0
1964	St. Louis Cardinals	NL	New York Yankees	AL	4 - 3
1965	Los Angeles Dodgers	NL	Minnesota Twins	AL	4 - 3
1966	Baltimore Orioles	AL	Los Angeles Dodgers	NL	4 - 0
1967	St. Louis Cardinals	NL	Boston Red Sox	AL	4 - 3
1968	Detroit Tigers	AL	St. Louis Cardinals	NL	4 - 3
1969	New York Mets	NL	Baltimore Orioles	AL	4 - 1
1970	Baltimore Orioles	AL	Cincinnati Reds	NL	4 - 1
1971	Pittsburgh Pirates	NL	Baltimore Orioles	AL	4 - 3
1972	Oakland Athletics	AL	Cincinnati Reds	NL	4 - 3
1973	Oakland Athletics	AL	New York Mets	NL	4 - 3
1974	Oakland Athletics	AL	Los Angeles Dodgers	NL	4 - 1
1975	Cincinnati Reds	NL	Boston Red Sox	AL	4 - 3
1976	Cincinnati Reds	NL	New York Yankees	AL	4 - 0
1977	New York Yankees	AL	Los Angeles Dodgers	NL	4 - 2
1978	New York Yankees	AL	Los Angeles Dodgers	NL	4 - 2
1979	Pittsburgh Pirates	NL	Baltimore Orioles	AL	4 - 3
1980	Philadelphia Phillies	NL	Kansas City Royals	AL	4 - 2
1981	Los Angeles Dodgers	NL	New York Yankees	AL	4 - 2
1982	St. Louis Cardinals	NL	Milwaukee Brewers	AL	4 - 3
1983	Baltimore Orioles	AL	Philadelphia Phillies	NL	4 - 1
1984	Detroit Tigers	AL	San Diego Padres	NL	4 - 1
1985	Kansas City Royals	AL	St. Louis Cardinals	NL	4 - 3
1986	New York Mets	NL	Boston Red Sox	AL	4 - 3
1987	Minnesota Twins	AL	St. Louis Cardinals	NL	4 - 3
1988	Los Angeles Dodgers	NL	Oakland Athletics	AL	4 - 1
1989	Oakland Athletics	AL	San Francisco Giants	NL	4 - 0
1990	Cincinnati Reds	NL	Oakland Athletics	AL	4 - 0
1991	Minnesota Twins	AL	Atlanta Braves	NL	4 - 3
1992	Toronto Blue Jays	AL	Atlanta Braves	NL	4 - 2
1993	Toronto Blue Jays	AL	Philadelphia Phillies	NL	4 - 2
1994	No Series				
1995	Atlanta Braves	NL	Cleveland Indians	AL	4 - 2
1996	New York Yankees	AL	Atlanta Braves	NL	4 - 2
1997	Florida Marlins	NL	Cleveland Indians	AL	4 - 3
1998	New York Yankees	AL	San Diego Padres	NL	4 - 0

World Series Most Valuable Players

YEAR	PLAYER	TEAM
1998	Scott Brosius	New York (AL)
1997	Livan Hernandez	Florida
1996	John Wetteland	New York (AL)
1995	Tom Glavine	Atlanta
1994	No Series	
1993	Paul Molitor	Toronto
1992	Pat Borders	Toronto
1991	Jack Morris	Minnesota
1990	Jose Rijo	Cincinnati
1989	Dave Stewart	Oakland
1988	Orel Hershiser	Los Angeles
1987	Frank Viola	Minnesota
1986	Ray Knight	New York (NL)
1985	Bret Saberhagen	Kansas City
1984	Alan Trammell	Detroit
1983	Rick Dempsey	Baltimore
1982	Darrell Porter	St. Louis
1981	Ron Cey	Los Angeles
	Pedro Guerrero	
	Steve Yeager	
1980	Mike Schmidt	Philadelphia
1979	Willie Stargell	Pittsburgh
1978	Bucky Dent	New York (AL)
1977	Reggie Jackson	New York (AL)
1976	Johnny Bench	Cincinnati
1975	Pete Rose	Cincinnati
1974	Rollie Fingers	Oakland
1973	Reggie Jackson	Oakland
1972	Gene Tenace	Oakland
1971	Roberto Clemente	Pittsburgh
1970	Brooks Robinson	Baltimore
1969	Donn Clendenon	New York (NL)
1968	Mickey Lolich	Detroit
1967	Bob Gibson	St. Louis
1966	Frank Robinson	Baltimore
1965	Sandy Koufax	Los Angeles
1964	Bob Gibson	St. Louis
1963	Sandy Koufax	Los Angeles
1962	Ralph Terry	New York (AL)
1961	Whitey Ford	New York (AL)
1960	Bobby Richardson	New York (AL)
1959	Larry Sherry	Los Angeles
1958	Bob Turley	New York (AL)
1957	Lew Burdette	Milwaukee
1956	Don Larsen	New York (AL)
1955	Johnny Podres	Brooklyn

The Season of Swat

Leonard Koppett

Even before the 1998 World Series began, commentators were telling the public that the spectacular home run race between Mark McGwire, who hit 70, and Sammy Sosa, who hit 66, had "brought baseball back" and made it popular again. No matter how often this idea was repeated, it was dead wrong. Baseball didn't "come back" because it had never been away.

When there was no World Series in 1994, and a shortened season in 1995 because of a labor-management struggle, fans certainly were upset and embittered. But as soon as play was resumed in 1995, in terms of attendance and every other measure of fan interest, things were back to normal within a year.

After all, the problem was the absence of games. Once they were taking place again, daily events and results took care of themselves. The seasons of 1996 and 1997 were filled with star performances and post-season drama, and were widely appreciated.

What McGwire of the Cardinals and Sosa of the Cubs did in 1998, therefore, was to bring baseball to a new peak of popularity. Climbing a higher mountain is quite different from being pulled out of a ditch. Babe Ruth's home runs had done that in the 1920s, generating new followers as well as stimulating old ones. He lifted The National Pastime to a new level, from which it continued to grow. Now the new home run champions raised the level of interest higher still.

But it wasn't just a coincidence that they shattered records set between 30 and 70 years ago.

The era of 1920-1962 set a certain standard for baseball offense, as measured by runs scored (9 to 10 runs a game for two teams) and aggregate batting average (.280). Then, for 30 years, from 1963 through 1992, scoring averaged 8.5 runs and the batting average was below .260.

Suddenly, in 1993, everything changed. Runs jumped back above 9.5 and the batting average to .267. Whether it was a livelier ball, as some believe, or something else, the new level has been like that ever since.

Fourteen times during the 1920-1962 period, some player hit 50 or more homers in a season. Nine different players did the hitting, reaching 61, 60, 59, 58 twice, 56, and 54 four times. In 1963-1992, only three men reached 50, no one hitting more than 52. Then, in the six seasons

Mark McGwire's Home Run Record Ball by Ball

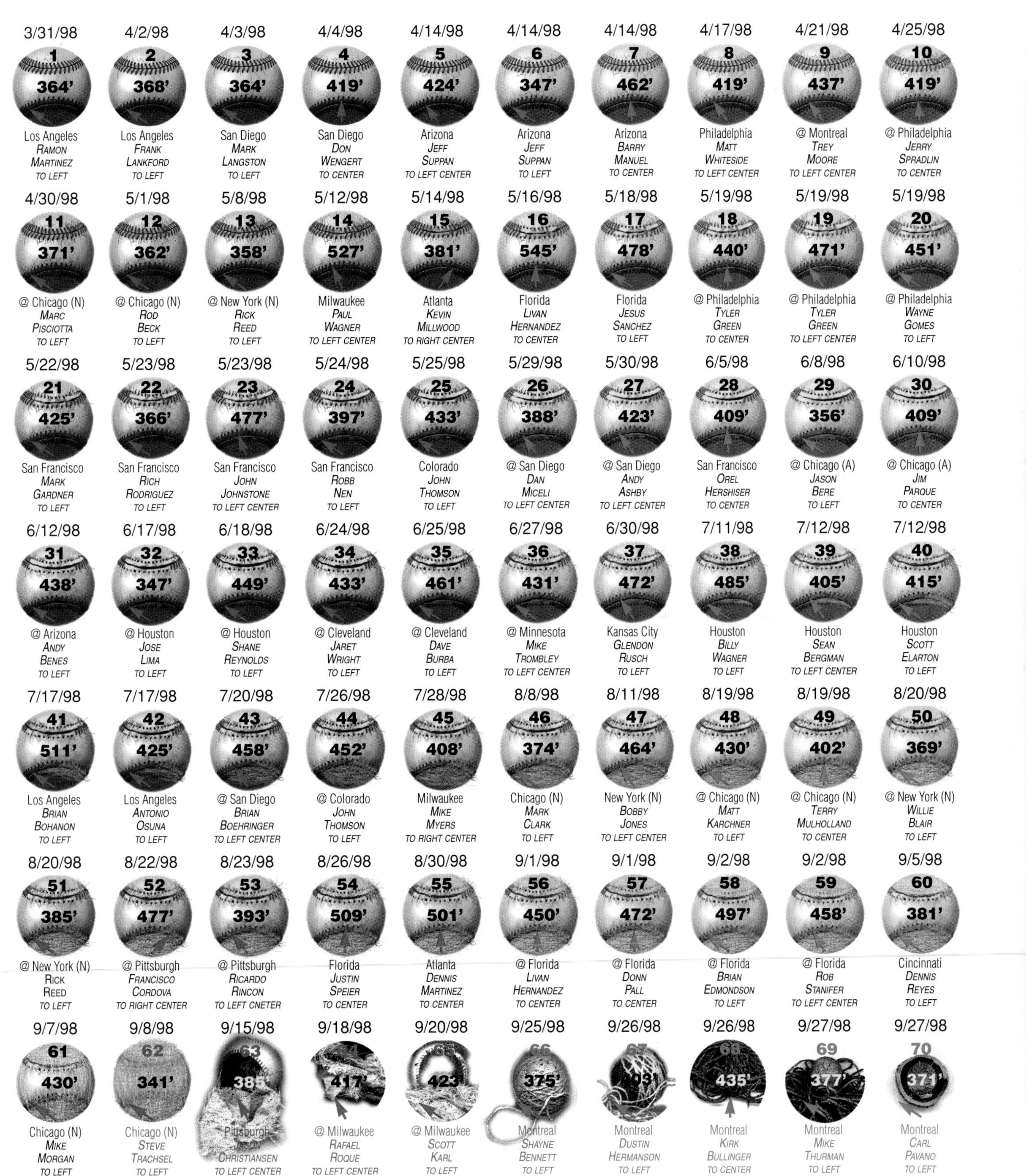

since 1993, six players have hit 50 or more nine times, getting 56 or more five times. The similarity between the two high-scoring eras, and contrasts with the period between them, is striking.

But the focus of excitement in 1998 was the two-man assault on the magic numbers of 60 (Ruth in 1927) and 61 (Roger Maris in 1961). McGwire had established his credentials long ago. His home run frequency (homers per at-bat) was like Ruth's, with no one else close, over an 11-year career. He hit 49 as a rookie and reached 58 in 1997. From 1998 Opening Day on, he was being asked if he thought he could match Maris.

Sosa had no such history, peaking at 40 homers in 1997. It wasn't until mid-season of 1998, when he started to match McGwire homer for homer, that their duel began monopolizing the sports pages. They were still even at 63 and again at 66.

When it was over, McGwire had his astounding 70, Sosa his unbelievable 66, and Seattle's Ken Griffey Jr. "only" 56 and Greg Vaughn of the Padres 50. Never before had more than two players reached 50 in the same season — but that had been done in 1938 and 1947 when there were only 16 teams and 1961 with 18. Since there are now 30 teams, four plus-50s is not so out of line. The startling thing is how far 70 and 66 are above 61.

Greg Vaughn of the Padres hit 50 home runs during the regular season.

Ruth had set the home run record at 29 in 1919, and it was written then that no one might ever do that again. The next year he hit 54, and the year after that 59. Six years later he hit 60, with relatively little fuss, since no one could expect he'd go still higher. In fact, the next season he was ahead of his 1927 pace until the last few weeks, and finished with 54.

Jimmy Foxx in 1932 and Hank Greenberg in 1938 came close with 58. After that, no one got more than 54 until Maris, in 1961. Then, only one year later, the offense was stifled for the next 30 years and 61 became unattainable under those conditions. That's what changed in 1963.

And the public, beyond question, prefers high-scoring baseball. Ruth's presence doubled baseball attendance overnight. After World War II, with night baseball and population growth, the numbers became much higher, but stayed relatively stagnant through the 1970s. In the 1990s, they have been about 25 percent higher (per game) than ever before.

That's why baseball didn't need "saving." It simply went higher than ever, and McGwire and Sosa deserve credit for taking it there. Every year can't be a peak, but the spotlight shone on the home run hitters in 1998 as never before.

Leonard Koppett covered baseball for many years for The New York Times. *He is in the writers wing of the Baseball Hall of Fame. His list of books reached 16 with the 1998 publication of* Koppett's Concise History of Baseball.

NOTES

Joe Gergen

AT THE FIRST World Series for which his team qualified, back in 1986 when he was a self-absorbed young slugger just entering his physical prime, Darryl Strawberry was singled out by the fans in Fenway Park. They chanted his name in derision as the Mets struggled to defeat the Red Sox in seven games. Even some of his own teammates snickered.

Twelve years later, several hundred Yankees fans who had made the trip to San Diego took up the chant following the final game of the team's sweep at Qualcomm Stadium. Only this time it was in tribute to the player who had undergone surgery for colon cancer on Oct. 3. The station that televised Yankees games broadcast the sight and sounds of the 1998 Series back to the metropolitan area, where Strawberry was resting at home.

This occurred after his Yankees teammates, led by David Wells, toasted the ailing star on TV and dedicated their victory to him. Even in absentia, "Straw" was a constant presence throughout the four games as the Yankees decided to have his number (39) sewn onto their caps, the ones adorned with World Series logos. . .

IN ANOTHER SILENT token of affection, Andy Pettitte printed "DAD" on his cap before taking the mound in Game Four. After pitching brilliantly, he went to a telephone and called his father, Tom, who had just been released from a Houston hospital one week after double-bypass surgery . . . For the Padres' Jim Leyritiz, the World Series started a lot better than it ended. Back in New York for Game One, two years after starring for the Yankees' 1996 world championship club, he led a camera crew onto the No. 4 train and made the subway ride to Yankee Stadium in his standard cowboy boots and hat. Then he was accorded a loud ovation in the pre-game introductions, a rarity for visitors. But with a chance to keep the Padres alive in Game Four, in the eighth inning he lined out to center with the bases loaded, extending his hitless streak to 10 at-bats. But he did nothing to damage his popularity in the Big Apple. . .

PERHAPS THE MOST relieved player in the World Series was Chuck Knoblauch, who was vilified in the tabloids after his brain cramp played a major role in the Yankees' loss to the Indians in Game Two of the ALCS. One headline writer referred to him as "Blauch-head." But the second baseman redeemed himself with a three-run homer in the seventh that tied the score in Game One, a .375 Series average and near-flawless defense. . .

ACTOR KEVIN COSTNER chatted up David Wells in the home-team clubhouse at Yankee Stadium and actor Charlie Sheen visited the pitcher in the visitors' locker room at Qualcomm Stadium. Wells received the marquee treatment outside nearby Point Loma High School where he played baseball and basketball. . .

JOE TORRE IS either clairvoyant or "the luckiest man on the face of the earth earth earth." Bypassing Chad Curtis and the gimpy Tim Raines, the Yankees' manager divided left field playing time between rookies Ricky Ledee and Shane Spencer. Spencer's double drove Sterling Hitchcock from the mound in Game Three, and Ledee bedeviled Kevin Brown while amassing six hits and driving in four runs. Their combined batting average was .538. . .

In contrast, Greg Vaughn, the San Diego left fielder whom the Yankees had acquired the previous summer only to see him flunk the club's physical exam, hit two home runs in Game One, then went hitless in his last 13 at-bats. . .

ONE YEAR after Orlando Hernandez — a physical therapist at a Cuban mental institution — slipped into the CNN studio in Havana to watch half-brother Livan pitch for Florida in the World Series, the man known as "El Duque" won Game Two for the Yankees, completing an odyssey one writer described as "raft to riches."

. . . Major League Baseball certainly was on its game in scheduling the pre-game ceremonies in New York and San Diego. Sammy Sosa opened the Series with the first pitch before Game One, and Mark McGwire closed the show with his toss before Game Four, bracketing a remarkable season in reflected glory. McGwire and Sosa's historic home run race highlighted what may have been baseball's greatest regular season, setting the stage for the 1998 Series. . .

WITH THE 1998 champion Yankees' regular-season record of 114 victories, the old best-team-ever debate flared anew. Listen to Padres batting coach Merv Rettenmund, who knows a lot about the last 30 years, at least: "I'll take the 1989 A's. They had the complete package." Rettenmund played for the Orioles in the early 1970s, the Reds in the mid-1970s and coached the A's of the late 1980's. He also slightly favors the early 1970s Orioles and the 1975 and 1976 Reds over the 1998 Yankees, but said the Yanks are "only" another World Series or two away from winning the argument. . . Exhibiting his usual class, Tony Gwynn celebrated his first visit to Yankee Stadium by strolling out to Monument Park in centerfield, then proceeding, fittingly, to hit a breathtaking two-run homer that temporarily stilled the New York crowd in Game One.

Joe Gergen is a sports writer for Newsday.